MARGARET MEAD

MARGARET MEAD

A Voice for the Century

c. 1

Robert Cassidy

UNIVERSE BOOKS
New York

B
MEAD, M.

For my mother, Clara Alfreda Nelson Cassidy

Published in the United States of America in 1982
by Universe Books
381 Park Avenue South, New York, N.Y. 10016

82 83 84 85 86 / 10 9 8 7 6 5 4 3 2 1

Printed in the United States of America

Cover photograph of Margaret Mead by Ken Heyman

Library of Congress Cataloging in Publication Data

Cassidy, Robert, 1946-
  Margaret Mead: a voice for the century.
  Bibliography: p.
  Includes index.
  1. Mead, Margaret, 1901-1978. 2. Anthropol-
ogists—United States—Biography. I. Title.
GN21.M36C37   301'.092'4 [B]   81-43435
ISBN 0-87663-376-9   AACR2

Contents

Acknowledgments

I would like to thank my agent, Dominick Abel, whose idea this book was; my wife Marsha and my daughters, who saw less of me than they might have wished; Arnold Dolin, for reasons only he could appreciate; my typists, Joan Allman and Elsie Phalen; Louis Barron, editorial director of Universe Books; and two members of Dr. Mead's staff, Amy Bard and Rosalind Lippel, who were extremely patient with me under duress, as well as Dr. Mead's bibliographer, Joan Gordan.

Grateful acknowledgment is made to *Redbook Magazine* for permission to quote from Margaret Mead's columns, "Questions about Children and Funerals . . ." (September 1963) and "Is Jealousy Innate? . . ." (July 1974). Copyright © Redbook Publishing Co. 1963, 1974. Used by permission.

1
A Citizen of the World

I have before me a packet of sugar with a sketch of Margaret Mead, drawn from a photograph by Ken Heyman. The sketch is none too flattering. It shows Mead in the last decade of her life, her close-cropped hair cut in bangs over her forehead, her eyes and mouth merely dark sockets. She is wearing a simple jacket over a high-necked dress, with a large—"oversize" might be the better word—brooch hanging from a chain around her neck. The artist missed the gleam of her blue eyes through her granny glasses and the smile that emanated from the corner of her mouth. But what is most extraordinary about this sugar packet is not its lack of artistic merit, but the very fact that it portrays an anthropologist, a member of a scientific profession barely known to the public. Surely the sugar company could have found an athlete, or a movie star, or some other celebrity, had it hoped to achieve instant recognition. Yet it is a measure of Mead's popularity that her portrait was used this way. Actually, it was not unusual for her to be idolized in this fashion. A restaurant in Cambridge's Harvard Square has a stained-glass portrait of her on the wall, along with such figures as Richard Nixon, Joe Namath, and Humphrey Bogart. Her likeness appears in a promotional ad in *Broadcasting* magazine for a summer camp for poor children sponsored by a Los Angeles radio station. She even had a *New Yorker* cartoon done about her. It shows an aboriginal chieftain preparing young boys for an initiation rite. "Rather than go into the details," he tells them, "I'm simply going to present each of you with a copy of this excellent book by Margaret Mead."

Mead was not only the preeminent anthropologist of her time, but from 1939 on, she was a figure of prominent importance in such fields as education, ecology, the women's movement, the Bomb, student uprisings, and on down the list of contemporary social and political issues. She maintained a firm base in science and anthropology, but always with the notion of relating these disciplines to concepts the typical person could understand. In sum, she was an intellectual and a scientist with a goal—to yoke science, the pursuit of knowledge for its own sake, with purpose.

It was precisely this blending of "knowledge joined to action" that distinguished Mead from so many of her staid colleagues and made her something of a national institution. Her talents, particularly in the latter part of her life, covered many fields. She was an academician, teacher, and education reformer, and her writings on the progressive education movement are as useful today as they were when written five decades ago. She served various presidents as a diplomat without portfolio on international commissions devoted to matters of ecology, nutrition, and the role of science and technology in the modern world. As a scientist, she held numerous official posts and contributed enormously to specialized areas, such as cross-cultural studies and the role of the scientist in the modern world. Most important, her ex-officio role as a critic and commentator upon contemporary mores—in such diverse areas as the family, the generation gap, sex, religious and moral issues, male-female relationships—transformed her into a kind of grandmotherly figure whose views were eagerly awaited by millions of Americans—and equally scorned by her detractors. No wonder *Time* named her "Mother of the World" in 1969.

How great was Mead's influence on American life? From any objective measure, considerable. As a scientist and scholar, her contribution was significant. She was without doubt one of the pioneers in anthropology in the United States, an achievement made all the more distinct because she was a woman in what had been a male-dominated field. Her trilogy of her initial South Seas voyages— *Coming of Age in Samoa, Growing Up in New Guinea,* and *Sex and Temperament in Three Primitive Societies*—cannot be ignored by scholars. Others may argue with Mead's conclusions, but her books on these

Oceanic expeditions stand firm in the literature of anthropology and alone would have placed Mead in the pantheon represented by Bronislaw Malinowski, Franz Boas, Ruth Benedict, Edward Sapir, and A. R. Radcliffe-Brown. When her other studies are added, notably *Male and Female, Balinese Character: A Photographic Analysis* (with Gregory Bateson), *Cooperation and Competition among Primitive Peoples, Continuities in Cultural Evolution,* and *New Lives for Old,* the sum is a significant body of work. Yet this is by no means the complete definition of Mead's scholarly pursuits. Indeed, the bibliography of her work from 1925 to 1975 alone runs to more than 100 printed pages. She was also one of the originators and developers of the concept of national character, a branch of anthropology that sought to analyze cultures on the basis of nationality; and, with Rhoda Métraux and others, she was a prime mover behind the study of culture at a distance, the analysis of the cultures of nation-states not immediately accessible to the scholar, which had a brief but useful role in our understanding of wartime Germany and Japan. She was an innovator in the use of photography as a tool of the cultural anthropologist, and her expertise in field work was well known throughout the profession. If there were a Hall of Fame for anthropologists, she'd be in it.

Her credentials were impeccable, and so extensive as to bear only summary here. She earned a bachelor's degree from Barnard College and her master's and Ph.D. degrees from Columbia University—to which were added a couple dozen honorary degrees and membership in the American Academy of Arts and Letters. Over the course of her life she served on the board of trustees of numerous colleges and universities and taught at such institutions of higher learning as Columbia, Vassar, New York University, Emory University, Yale, the New School for Social Research, the University of Cincinnati, and the Menninger Clinic. She helped found the urban anthropology department at NYU in 1965 and created the anthropology department at Fordham's liberal arts college in 1968. Among her many affiliations, appointments, and positions, Mead was at one time president of the American Anthropological Association, the Society for General Systems Research, the Anthropological Film Institute, the World Society for Ekistics, the Scientists' Institute for Public Information, the Society for Applied Anthropology, and the American Association for the Advancement of Science. This last is particularly significant in that Mead was the first AAAS president to be elected (in 1974) by a vote of the general membership, an indication of her standing in the scientific community. Her work also included membership on the U.S. Commission on the Year 2000, the AAAS Committee on Science in the Promotion of Human Welfare, the Academy of Religion and Mental Health, and the Teilhard Center for the Future of Mankind. Throughout the years, she maintained her base at the American Museum of Natural History in New York, where she became assistant curator in 1926; associate curator, 1942; curator, 1964; and curator emeritus, 1969. The culmination of her association with the museum came in 1971 with the opening of the Hall of the Peoples of the Pacific, a tribute to Mead and her work in Oceania.

Yet the interesting thing about Mead's scientific work was not only its vast dimension, but its purpose. As her friend and colleague Barry Commoner said, "Dr. Mead's contribution to science in general—to the broad overall field of the sciences—is her pioneering work in setting the sciences into relationship to human life." It was precisely this goal of melding science with humanism that propelled Mead into her work in national and international affairs during the latter part of her life. At the beginning of World War II she was appointed to a national commission studying American food habits, work which led to additional postwar studies on hunger and malnutrition at home and abroad. Mead became expert on the relationship between technology and economic development, heading various international commissions in an effort to determine how the countries of the emerging Third World could be brought into the 20th century—a problem that Mead, as a scholar of cultural development who emphasized matters of mental health, was uniquely suited to explore. As a scientist and humanist, she carried her interests over to city planning, becoming one of the major proponents of ekistics, the science of human settlements, and to the quality of life—well before many of these issues were fashionable. Her concern for human welfare carried religious and moral connotations that emanated from her deep ethical beliefs and that prompted her leadership in such groups as the World Council of Churches. She was a firm believer in the need for a single world language that would provide a common base of communications to unify all people. She was not hesitant about making known her opinions on specific religious and moral issues, such as nuclear arms proliferation, the role of women in the churches, abortion, genetic engineering, and the rights of the terminally ill.

Her most important role, however, was as an interpreter of world events and trends to the American people. Beginning with her first major published work, Mead attempted to show the significance of these larger world and cultural patterns to the lives of ordinary Americans. Sometimes her pronouncements were greeted with disdain and even anger. When *Coming of Age in Samoa* was published in 1928, the American Legion condemned the YMCA for having the scurrilous author of that "sex book" on the YMCA board of directors—even though it turned out that the Margaret Mead on the YMCA board was a different Margaret Mead. Many years later, the governor of Florida, Claude R. Kirk, called her a "dirty old lady" for her views on the decriminalization of marijuana, and Martha Mitchell, the wife of Attorney General John Mitchell, called her a "spook." Rarely did such criticism bother her.

She responded through her writings and speeches. In one of the first studies of national character, *And Keep Your Powder Dry: An Anthropologist Looks at America,* she tried to explain what it was that made Americans unique. She was a prolific writer on civil rights and race, always placing her thoughts within the context of cultural analysis, as in her "talking book" with writer James Baldwin, *A Rap on Race.* She wrote on ways to improve education in such books as *The School in American Culture* and on the process of neighborhood development and community problem-solving in *The Wagon and the Star* (with Muriel Brown). Her many articles on the environment, energy, and economic development placed her in the forefront of American thinking on these subjects. She liked nothing more than to shake people up with a radical proposal, such as her call for mandatory national service to replace the draft or her suggestion for a "trial" or "student" marriage. Some of her proposals were ill-conceived, impractical, or politically unfeasible, such as her idea of paying students to attend college. But many others are as valid today as they were when Mead first proposed them.

She was a "liberated woman" who made headlines when she kept her maiden name after her first marriage. Two years after her death in 1978, a couple of women started a line of trading cards portraying leading feminists, and Mead was named one of seventy-two "Supersisters," along with Bella Abzug, Gloria Steinem, Ruby Dee, and Doriot Anthony Dwyer, principal flutist with the Boston Symphony Orchestra. Yet she was never entirely comfortable being labeled a

feminist and at times had harsh words for Friedanesque cultists. A
traditionalist in many ways, especially in her relationship with her
daughter Mary Catherine, she abhorred being called "manlike" and
prided herself on her femininity. "My mother thinks being a female is
marvelous," daughter Cathy said in 1972. "She wouldn't be a man for
anything." Mead never failed to remind others that it was because she
was a woman, and therefore able to enter the sacred and mysterious
world reserved to women, that she was able to conduct her first field
expedition among the young girls of Samoa. "I've never been an
imitation man," she said. "I've done things in my work only a woman
can do. I've studied and observed children in areas where no man
would be tolerated."

It was in her role as counselor to the American family—America's
grandmother, if you will—that Mead made her most profound mark
on American society. For seventeen years, from 1961 until her death in
1978, her monthly column in *Redbook* magazine (written with Rhoda
Métraux) offered solace, information, advice, and common sense to
millions of American women. She understood women, and they in turn
looked up to her as a model woman. She enjoyed answering their
questions on a wide range of subjects: Is there any equivalent to toilet
training among primitive peoples? Are there really so many more
youth crimes today than in previous eras? What do the games children
play reveal about human nature? Is jealousy innate? As an anthropologist, a mother, and a grandmother, what do you think are the
qualities most valuable to a mother in helping children toward
maturity? Are you opposed to coeducation? Do men have a fathering
instinct? Do you agree with psychologists who believe that children
are born knowing how to love but are taught to hate? In addition,
articles by or about her appeared in numerous other women's and
general-interest magazines—*Look, McCall's, Cosmopolitan, U.S. News &
World Report, Chatelaine, Parents Magazine, The New York Times Magazine,
The New Yorker*. She treated her readers as equals. She was once asked
to rewrite an article for *Harper's* because the editors felt it was too
difficult for their readers to understand; Mead refused and had it
published in *Redbook,* without change or a single complaint from a
reader as to its difficulty.

She often ventured into uncharted territory when she talked to
women about the Pill, abortion, sex, and marriage. She took up the
problems of alienated youth—the so-called generation gap—in an

effort to show the cultural aspects of this particularly gnawing problem faced by parents in the 1960s and 1970s. At the same time, she was concerned about old people and grandparents and detailed her thoughts on how the elderly should be integrated into society. She outraged conservationists with some of her ideas, notably the suggestion of a trial or student marriage for young people, as differentiated from a mature or parental marriage in which children would be conceived. She had firm thoughts about premarital sex among teenagers, divorce, child custody, motherhood, breast feeding, and practically every other issue touching the American family. Indeed, it could be said that, for most of the last two decades, Margaret Mead helped shape the American family's image of itself. That she herself was thrice married and thrice divorced, a mother, and a grandmother, seemed only to add to her credibility among her readers.

Even up to the last year of her life, when cancer limited her activities, she kept a schedule that would exhaust a decathlon champion. Her day would start at five in the morning, when she would read books, articles, the newspapers, and student theses, then move into her own material, polishing an article for *Redbook* or the introduction to a book. She treasured those early hours alone, just as she enjoyed the companionship of others at concerts and parties. By ten she would have consulted with her staff and made any last-minute changes of schedule. Then she would be off to lunch with a women's group, a colleague, or one of her editors. If she was not traveling, she would work at her office in the afternoon, teach her classes at Columbia and Fordham, meet with students, and prepare the talk she would give that night. Dinner might be taken at the apartment she shared with Rhoda Métraux, or at one of her favorite restaurants. After the speech, she would return to her home and read till after midnight.

Her itinerary for the week of February 13 to 20, 1970, is indicative of the kind of schedule she kept:

Friday, February 13: Meet with students in the morning. Lunch with editor at *McCall's*. Dinner and talk at Fairleigh Dickinson University, Rutherford, New Jersey. Return to New York by car, take 3:23 A.M. train to Washington.

Saturday, February 14: Confer all day with State Department officials on issues facing youths. Informal dinner with friends. Fly to Philadelphia.

Sunday, February 15: Breakfast with the trustees of the Academy of Natural Sciences. Press conference and public lecture. Afternoon talk at University of Pennsylvania conference on population and environment. Return to Washington.

Monday, February 16: Meet all day with Ekistics Society. Return to New York.

Tuesday, February 17: Classes at Columbia and Fordham.

Wednesday, February 18: Tape "The Mike Douglas Show" in Philadelphia. Evening banquet in Atlantic City to receive the 1970 American Education Award from the American Association of School Administrators.

Thursday, February 19: Teach 9:30 A.M. class. Lunch with Nigel Calder, the British scientist. Moderate afternoon panel on fertility control and women's careers at the New York Academy of Sciences.

In the period from September 1962 to June 1963, she participated in the following activities: the London conference of the Pugwash group (scientists from both hemispheres concerned about nuclear disasters); The Fifth International Food Conference, in New York, where she gave a paper on nutrition; a conference in Montreal on women's roles in the International Cooperation Year; the Third Unofficial Soviet-American Conference of Public Figures, held in Andover, Massachusetts (just as the Cuban missile crisis broke out, incidentally); a theater trip to London; a two-week sojourn at the University of Cincinnati, where she lectured in the psychiatry department; plus her usual work at the American Museum of Natural History, her teaching at Columbia, and her family considerations. She maintained this pace for fifty years and, amazingly, worked even more vigorously when in the field. It is no wonder that when Jean Houston once asked her which of the seven deadly sins was hers, she replied greed—greed for new experiences.

She might have become an artist or a poet. She once told T. George Harris, "I was talented, you know, without genius, but I could write and I could paint." Yet she knew she didn't have what it takes to make it in the creative world, especially after comparing herself with her college roommate, the poet Léonie Adams. "We live in a society where you can achieve in the arts only if you are superlatively good," she told Harris, "and science has plenty of room for middle-range achievement."

This uncharacteristically self-denigrating statement belied Mead's true talent with the printed—and spoken—word. Her trick was simple: She wrote in English. Oh, she was capable of writing the most verbose, convoluted prose imaginable and sometimes did so when addressing technical audiences. But when she wrote for the lay reader, she was clear, precise, and lively—as a rereading of the first six pages of *Coming of Age in Samoa*, that magnificent description of a typical day in the village of Tau, attests. Her longtime editor, John Willey, said after her death, "I realized she writes as she speaks—very fluently and very fast." In the preface to *Aspects of the Present*, a collection of her *Redbook* articles, the editor-in-chief of that magazine, Sey Chassler, says of Mead that "clarity and sanity were her goals" in writing and that she took editorial criticism "with grace and charm." She was known to be able to complete a book in 24 days, using an electric typewriter, never dictating. Usually, though, she took her time. It was her practice to mull over an idea in speeches or public appearances before putting it into final form, a habit she learned early, after she had written the field-study part of *Coming of Age in Samoa* and was lecturing in the United States. It occurred to her that the questions her audiences asked would be shared by her readers, so she added two chapters on the application of her Samoan studies to contemporary American adolescents. Those chapters added enormously to the popularity of the book and established Mead as a special kind of anthropologist and writer.

Mead would have made a fine writer no matter what field she chose. (I doubt she would have made a good politician, a career possibility she flirted with briefly. She was too true to herself to bear making the kinds of compromises a politician must learn to accept, and her three divorces ruled the field out anyway.) Although she was by no means a humorous writer, she occasionally displayed wit. She once wrote that "life in the 20th century is like a parachute jump: You have to get it right the first time." In "Styles of American Womanhood," she described the traditional division of labor in American households, with the men taking care of everything *outside* the home and the women taking care of everything *inside*. The conflict arose over the garbage. "Garbage is ambiguous," she said. "Garbage originates indoors and goes outdoors. Who does it belong to?"

She was much more biting in her personal appearances and interviews. When asked by an interviewer from the *East West Journal*, a counterculture publication, what she thought of macrobiotic food, Mead replied that "when you eat macrobiotic food, you aren't eating food, you're eating an ideology. I prefer to eat food." At Radcliffe College in 1969, she spoke out against coeducation: "Twenty-four hours a day with boys can be appalling. It's bad enough to have breakfast every day with your husband." On the subject of husbands, Mead was often asked how she could counsel people about marriage when she herself had been married and divorced three times. "I *don't* consider my marriages as failures!" she told an interviewer from *Cosmopolitan* in 1977. "It's idiotic to assume that because a marriage ends, it's failed"—it was simply the end of a union. On sex, a subject that interested most those interviewers who least understood her work, she would occasionally lose her temper, as she did with a questioner who seemed intent on taking the mystery out of sex. "Sex is not like beefsteak!" Mead exclaimed. Nor was she afraid to deflate fads and popular myths, including those she herself propagated. Talking to a reporter about the generation gap, she noted that even young children today know about such complex things as open-heart surgery. "On the other hand, there are things people used to know that this generation hasn't learned, such as how to spell."

Her skill as a lecturer was unrivaled. She would walk to the microphone (aided by her trusty thumbstick, which she needed to support an ankle that she had broken several times) and sit before it, check to make sure everyone in the hall could hear her, and then discourse for an hour without reference to notes or a printed text, all the while including examples from today's news, her latest field trip, a recent lunch with a Nobel laureate, and gossip and tidbits she had extracted from her hosts on the way in from the airport. "I never give the same one twice—I'd die of boredom if I did," she said. Invariably she would allude to her Oceanic studies, comparing contemporary attitudes on breastfeeding or childbirth to those of the Mundugumor or the Arapesh, throwing light on the problems of education or ecology by reference to the Manus. Sometimes she would get so caught up in her own ideas she would forget her audience. David Dempsey tells a probably apocryphal story of her giving an extended clinical analysis of sexual deviation among the Tchambuli to a group of theologians. "The talk," said Dempsey, "was well received." She liked to open the floor to questions, and it was here that Mead excelled. Because she was as good a listener as she was a speaker, she managed to extract something valuable from even the most stupid or inane question, thereby not only educating the audience, but challenging the next questioner to top the last. She had the same facility in panel discussions. She would sit back for a half-hour or so, then sweep in and tie a whole conversation together in a few well-conceived paragraphs, giving every previous speaker full credit for his contribution, but adding—through a thoughtful question or brilliant insight—some new and exciting idea that made every participant look considerably more intelligent than he really was. As her longtime friend and colleague Rhoda Métraux said, "She had the rare gift of being able to take from others and to make what she had taken her own without in any way diminishing the individuality or worth of those who worked with her."

This keen ability to synthesize thought was by no means her only intellectual acuity. According to Jean Houston, a psychologist and director of the Foundation for Mind Research in Pomona, New York, Mead had one of the most "filled" minds of any person Houston had ever come into contact with professionally, using more of her intellectual capacity than anyone Houston had ever known. Mead also possessed the best hand-eye coordination of any person Houston had ever tested, an attribute that probably goes back to Mead's early training by her paternal grandmother. Moreover, according to Houston, Mead possessed the rare capacity for synesthesia, or cross sensing. She could perceive the same sensation in more than one sense: She could "touch" an aroma, hear color, see sound. She once described Houston's voice as a brush, somewhere between a pig's bristles and a silk brush—but definitely not nylon, she said.

Mead came as close as anyone to describing her own intellectual capacities when she was asked to name the most stimulating person she had ever met. Her reply—John G. Winant, United States ambassador to Great Britain during World War II—is perhaps surprising, considering the many stellar people she knew, but her explanation could also be turned into an analysis of her own gifts: "He combined an extraordinary intellectual speed, so that one never had to pause or rephrase an idea, with a tremendous sense of moral responsibility, so that all quick solutions had to be tested, turned over and examined from all sides. One could actually *see* his extraordinary mental processes at work as one of his hands moved with the speed of thought while the other almost fumbled in the efforts to slow down and consider all the consequences. Every conversation with him was both stimulating and momentous."

Yet she was no aloof intellectual, although to some she might have seemed that way. In an otherwise flattering article, for example, Gail Sheehy paints Mead as something of a cold fish in her dealings with friends. But most other evidence contradicts this impression. She was generous and at the same time demanding with her own time, particularly when dealing with students and interviewers; perhaps it was because she did not suffer fools lightly that she seemed harsh in her ways. She kept friends for life and maintained correspondence with people she knew as far back as the fourth grade. Her friend from Bucks County, Julian W. Gardy, wrote upon her return to her old stomping grounds years later, "I thought, as I sat listening to her chat, what a gift she has for holding on to people no matter how many years and how many miles and how many new interests come between." She was equally generous with her money, putting much of her earnings from royalties into grants for anthropology students to conduct field research. She also donated her time and lectures to worthwhile groups. It could hardly be said that she lived an extravagant life, as one look at her clothes would quickly reveal.

Her fame, however, occasionally cut into her relationships with fellow scientists. Early in her career, for instance, a critic charged that she had misunderstood the kinship patterns among the Manus. Mead responded by writing *Kinship in the Admiralty Islands*, probably the most thorough study of kinship organization in a primitive society up to that time (1934). She was the only anthropologist required to join the American Federation of Television and Radio Artists, and there were those in the profession who would have preferred Mead to stick close to her desk and never go to see Johnny Carson. Her off-the-cuff remarks were dismissed by some as unprofessional, while the critic David Brudnoy referred to her pithy statements not as "meaty Meadisms," but as "Meadiocrities." As one fellow ethnologist said of her, "Everyone talks about Margaret Mead but nobody does anything about her." Yet there was a kind of grudging admiration for her. "The professional anthropologist is liable to react to the mention of Margaret Mead's name with, at best, a smile, and probably with some more positive expression of distaste," said anthropologist Peter Worsley. "Yet few of them have attempted to analyze her work, or to make it clear exactly what it is they object to." Her facility with language and her ability to cut to the core of a problem may have made some of her suggestions seem simplistic, but she was more often correct than not. Once, in the 1960s, while serving on a commission in India, Mead suggested that the farmers preferred their old wooden plows to the new steel plows because the wooden ones broke, giving the farmer the opportunity to make contact with the local carpenter, whose wife would give the farmer's wife a sari on feast days. Of course, Mead was right, and measures had to be taken to ensure the continuity of that cultural exchange.

One of her earliest critics was Gregory Bateson, her third husband. In 1932, when Mead and her second husband Reo Fortune visited Bateson at his digs on the middle Sepik River in New Guinea, Bateson greeted Mead with a jibe at *Growing Up in New Guinea*. After Mead explained the point to him, however, Bateson changed his mind. "He was later to remark that anthropologists who had read my work but did not know me tended to doubt my conclusions because they could not allow for the speed with which I worked," Mead explained, in her typically immodest, but accurate, way.

Mead may not have been loved by all her colleagues, but she did win their respect. As one fellow anthropologist said of her, "None of us knows what really lies ahead, not even Margaret Mead. But I assure you, if there is a committee in charge, she will be on it."

For fifty years, Mead was the bellwether of anthropology both in the United States and abroad, a figure of international prominence, a writer whose books were bestsellers and which still sell in the tens of thousands each year. Most likely she would have made a name for herself in whatever profession she chose. Yet fate opened the door to anthropology, and through it she stepped.

2
To the South Seas

Judging by the evidence of her early life, Margaret seemed headed in some unusual direction, but anthropology, then only a budding science in America, was hardly a likely prospect. In one respect, though, her choice of careers was not at all accidental. She seemed always ready to capitalize whenever opportunity crossed her path. Where others might have squandered these chances, she recognized their potential and used them to the greatest advantage. "Get the distaff ready, and God will send the flax" her grandmother used to say, and that became a motto for young Margaret.

She was born in Philadelphia, December 18, 1901, the eldest of four children: Richard, born 1904; Elizabeth, born 1909, and Priscilla, born 1911. (Another sister, Katherine, died in infancy.) Her parents were educators. Edward Sherwood Mead, a professor at the Wharton School of Finance and Commerce at the University of Pennsylvania, was an expert on the use of waste products in coal mining and, for someone with so much training in finance, a notoriously bad investor whose poor luck gave him an excuse to plead poverty whenever he found it convenient. Emily Fogg Mead was educated at the University of Chicago and conducted research on Italian immigrant families, eventually earning a doctorate—quite a distinction for a woman in those days. Mead's grandfathers died before she was born, and she does not seem to have liked her maternal grandmother, Elizabeth

Bogart Fogg. Most of her adulation is saved for her paternal grandmother, Martha Ramsay Mead, whom Mead called "the most decisive influence in my life." Grandmother Mead, the wife of a school superintendent, had herself been a high school principal and did not hesitate to put her theories of education to work on Margaret. She had Margaret chart the habits of her younger sisters, held daily lessons for her, made her build a herbarium to learn about plants, and in general supervised the child's schooling—itself a godsend, since the family moved around so much during Margaret's school-age years that her formal education was often neglected.

More important than the actual training and education she received from her mother and grandmother was the belief they instilled in her that a woman could have a profession of her own, at least in addition to the traditional role of wife and homemaker. Her mother, a suffragette and campaigner for social causes, was known for her peculiarities. She painted the kitchen ceiling of their farmhouse, for example, something no woman in Bucks County, Pennsylvania, had ever done. She encouraged Margaret and the other children to play with children of all backgrounds and classes in order to drive racial and class prejudices from their minds. The result, said Mead, was that she was "brought up within my own culture two generations ahead of my time." The net effect was that she "took pride in being unlike other children and in living in a household that was itself unique."

Mead's upbringing and early education can be seen in retrospect to have provided her with valuable tools for her career as an anthropologist. She was taught early to observe closely the behavior and peculiarities of others, to work with her hands, to paint, to dance and appreciate music, to cook and sew and care for children—skills that would serve her well in the field years later. Yet when she graduated from high school in Doylestown, Pennsylvania, in 1918, her future was far from certain. For a while, her father wanted her to go to nursing school, causing young Margaret to stage what she later called one of her few fits of feminist rage. Then there was talk of going to Wellesley College, near Boston, but that was soon put aside in favor of DePauw, her father's alma mater in Greencastle, Indiana, which she entered in the fall of 1919. After one wholly unsatisfactory year at DePauw, she transferred to Barnard College, the women's college of Columbia University. Thus began a relationship with Columbia that was to span nearly six decades.

In New York, Mead fell in with a group of talented, sophisticated, intellectual young women known collectively as the Ash Can Cats, who shared her interest in literature (especially poetry), theater, and social causes. They marched together in the spring of 1921 to protest the trial of Sacco and Vanzetti, wrote editorials and letters to campus newspapers, talked about men, sex, and Freudian psychology, held dinner parties, and organized a coeducational lecture society, with Margaret as president.

As for her studies, Mead's beginning in English literature soon soured when it became apparent that she would never become a great creative writer like her friend Léonie Adams. Moreover, the influence of her mother and grandmother, both students of human behavior, pushed her in the general direction of the social sciences. The only question was, which one? For a while she leaned toward sociology, then psychology; indeed, she eventually wrote her master's thesis in psychology on the children of the Italian immigrants in Hammonton, New Jersey, that her mother had studied. In the end, the decision came down to a choice between senior-year elective courses—a philosophy course, or an anthropology course taught by the white-maned department chairman, Franz Boas.

Boas, a physicist by training, had suffered anti-Semitic persecution and discrimination in his native Germany, though not willingly—he bore the scars of a duel allegedly instigated by a racial slur. Emigrating to the United States, he conducted research among the Eskimos of Baffin Land and Hudson Bay and the Kwakiutl of the Pacific Northwest, famous for their custom of potlatch. In 1893 he organized the highly popular anthropology exhibit at the World's Columbian Exposition in Chicago, but was sorely disappointed when he failed to get the directorship of the Field Museum of Natural History. Eventually he wound up at Columbia University, where he established an anthropology department with the goal of investigating the essentially unified nature of the human race—not, as was the more accepted role of the social sciences at that time, to churn out apologetics proving the relative superiority of European–American (that is, "white") cultures. To this end, Boas thought it essential to study primitive peoples, whose very "purity" would provide insights into the basics of human nature. It was for this reason that he impressed his students with a sense of urgency, lest these primitive tribes be overwhelmed by Western acculturation before being chron-icled. It was Boas, with his message of urgency, and Ruth Benedict, later Mead's closest friend and confidante, who persuaded Mead to become an anthropologist. Mead recalled a lunch with Benedict, in which the subject of her future came up. Benedict said, "Professor Boas and I have nothing to offer but an opportunity to do work that matters." As Mead noted in *Blackberry Winter*, "That settled it for me. Anthropology had to be done *now*. Other things could wait."

Actually, some things could not wait. All the while Mead was away at college, she was engaged to a Pennsylvania State College theology student four years her elder named Luther Cressman, whom she had met in 1918. They were married in September 1923, and Luther continued his theological studies as a graduate fellow at the General Theological Seminary and served as part-time pastor of a church in Brooklyn, while Margaret finished her master's work, under a graduate fellowship in sociology. Her dream of raising six children was shattered when a doctor informed her she could never have children. The freedom from pregnancy, however, released her from the sedentary life of the parsonage and allowed her to consider field work, a possibility made all the more tantalizing when she attended a meeting of the British Association for the Advancement of Science in Toronto in the summer of 1924. There she met working anthropologists like T. F. McIlwraith, who was studying the Bella Bella, and Edward Sapir, who was working on Jungian psychology. "At Toronto, I learned the delight of intellectual arguments among peers," wrote Mead. "I, too, wanted to have a 'people' on whom I could base my intellectual life."

She soon had her chance. Boas, in his effort to build the emerging field of anthropology into a methodical discipline, wanted his students to conduct studies to measure the relationship between the development of the individual and the distinctive features of the culture in which the person was raised. Whenever he could, Boas would send another budding anthropologist off to the field to test one of his "ideas," as he called them. When his secretary and editorial assistant, Ruth Bunzel, decided she was sick of typing and demanded a real challenge, Boas shuffled her off to study the Zuñi. The result was her book *The Pueblo Potter*. To young Margaret Mead he assigned the task of determining whether the "storm and stress" common to adolescents in Western culture was to be found in primitive cultures. In other words, were these adolescent "troubles" peculiar to Western culture, or an inherent aspect of adolescence? Boas also wanted the answers to specific questions: How did young girls in primitive societies react to the constraints of custom—with a rebellious spirit, as in Western culture, or in some other way? Was it true that primitive girls are excessively bashful? Under what circumstances did they develop crushes and other forms of romantic love?

Although she would have preferred to study cultural change, Mead, with her interest in psychology, found these questions challenging. But she and Boas had vastly different ideas as to how and where her studies should be carried out. "Papa Franz" looked at his slight, 23-year-old graduate student and decided that the only safe place for her was with an Indian tribe in the American West. Mead, feisty as ever, was equally determined to study the natives of the Tuamotu Islands, in the South Seas, and even managed to cajole her father into paying for the trip. In the end, a compromise was reached: Mead would study adolescent girls in Polynesia, but on an island in the American Samoa group, where she could be watched by the U.S. Department of the Navy.

In the summer of 1925, Mead and Luther Cressman vacationed together in New England. Then he got ready to sail for Europe to continue his studies, and Mead left by train for San Francisco and the ship that would take her to Pago Pago, the administrative center of American Samoa.

It is difficult today to imagine what it was like for a five-foot-two-and-a-half inch, 98-pound woman, who had never so much as been aboard a ship, stayed a night in a hotel, or spoken a foreign language to any foreigner on foreign soil, to venture forth on such an expedition in the year 1925. For a young woman—a married woman, traveling alone no less—to do so, even in the heyday of the Jazz Age, was quite extraordinary. Certainly U.S. Navy officials did not want her there, for if anything happened to her, they would be blamed—and there would be all that paperwork to complete, in triplicate. Shortly after her arrival in Pago Pago, she was given an audience with the American governor of the islands, a plantation-type straight out of Somerset Maugham (indeed, Mead spent her first night at the hotel where Maugham had set his story "Rain"), who informed her that he had never learned the language and would never learn it, and that neither would she. This prediction nearly proved true, for despite the tutoring of a native girl, Mead had the nastiest time mastering the tongue.

Mead herself must have harbored some fears about the expedition.

Certainly she was aware that the Samoans, while they could be expected to be primitive—in the sense of being different, not necessarily less complex—were hardly savages, and certainly not cannibals. (That experience would wait for later voyages.) And though a half-century later she would write that a field anthropologist's first lesson is to learn "to expect almost anything, however strange," she did come in for a few surprises. She forgot to pack a lamp to work at night, and only the last-minute reminder of a friend in Honolulu saved her that embarrassment and inconvenience. She was told not to wear silk because it would rot and packed six cotton dresses, only to find all the nonnative women wearing silk dresses. In Pago Pago, she was shocked to discover, the Samoans all carried black umbrellas to guard against the sun and most of them wore unbecoming overblouses (of cotton!), with only the dancers who greeted her ship in the traditional *lava-lava*, or grass skirt. During her "training" period with her tutor, a native girl named Fa'alava, and later at the home of Fa'amotu, the daughter of one of the local chiefs, she was indoctrinated into the culture, learning to eat the strange foods—taro, land crabs, wild pigeon, breadfruit—prepared for her, suffering the embarrassment of having everyone else wait to eat till she finished her meal, learning to "pass kava" (a ceremony equivalent to British high tea), sitting on her legs native-style until she could hardly walk, then having to repay her hosts' courtesy by dancing Samoan-style—*lava-lava* and all—far into the night. She had to learn how to bathe herself in an outdoor shower, in full view of the whole village, by holding a kind of sarong around herself and slipping her clothes off underneath. She was introduced to a visiting chief from British Samoa, who proceeded to rhapsodize about the free and easy sex life in his portion of the world and informed Mead with a leer, "White women have such nice fat legs." She managed to extricate herself from this delicate situation by informing the chief that she was not of his rank and therefore not worthy of his favors. She even survived a hurricane by huddling, with a child on top of her, in a bathtub.

Once Mead was ensconced in the tiny village of Tau, in the Manu'a islands group (after a hazardous passage over the reef, with the seasick anthropologist bobbing like a top in a tin canoe), she settled down to the day-to-day work of a field anthropologist—recording ceremonies, observing daily activities and family relationships, and talking with the subjects of her study, the Samoan adolescents. But in the larger sense, her research in Tau was Mead's first step in a lifelong study: Is human nature rigid and unyielding, or pliable and malleable, depending on one's culture?

For nine months, she studied, wrote her field notes, took photographs, and lived the life of a Samoan girl—her size at last proving to be an asset. She learned how the Samoan family was organized, with infants being cared for by their older brothers and sisters, themselves only six or seven years of age. Children were free to move from household to household in search of the most comfortable living arrangement while still belonging to the larger family, the village—a far cry from the "nuclear" arrangement in Western families. She catalogued the village hierarchy—the *fono*, or assembly of headmen, or *matais*, who are essentially the village chiefs; the *aumaga*, the closely knit young men's association; and the *taupo*, or ceremonial princess of each house—and observed its ceremony, particularly noting how dance serves as a means to allow children to overcome their shyness by "acting out" with precocious or individualized ways of behavior. She took note of the way that Samoans displayed virtually no sense of comparison, but judged everything in black and white, good or bad, never in shades of gray. She learned that the most reprehensible trait among Samoans was to be deemed *faisili*, or "stuck up," and that judgments about one's character were made on the basis of relative age, not some adult ideal, so that boys and girls of nine or ten years old were expected to behave accordingly, not like young men or young ladies. She observed how Samoans resort to *musu*, an inability or unwillingness to explain an act or its motivation, as if they were shrugging their shoulders and saying "Search me"—a reaction Mead attributed to the tight quarters and lack of privacy in Samoan society.

But Mead's most remarkable observations—the material that would secure her position in anthropology—had to do with the courtship patterns among Samoan adolescents. Love among the Samoans was quite different from that which a Philadelphia-born, Barnard-educated woman was used to. Clandestine moonlight affairs under the palm trees, published elopements (called *avaga*), surreptitious rape by a supposedly sleep-walking man (called *moetotolo*), the use of a "John Alden" figure (called a *soa*) to plead for a girl's love—these and other strange rituals differentiated Samoan love from Western courtship patterns. Monogamy, exclusiveness, jealousy—none of these "civilized" concepts were valued or indeed even understood by the Samoans. Divorce could take place simply by having one of the marriage partners "go home," whereupon the marriage would "pass away." It was all truly exotic, and therein lay its tremendous attraction.

Coming of Age in Samoa, the book Mead wrote upon her return to the United States in 1926 (and which was published two years later after she had already departed for her second field study), quickly became a best seller. Not only was it beautifully written, but the subject of sexual relationships among "primitive" girls clearly piqued the interest of a society barely emerging from the Victorian age. Today's reader would find nothing to shock his sensibilities, and even for its times the book was modest in its discussion of sexual mores. Still, the subject matter, coupled with the accessible, novelistic style so unusual for an anthropologist, contributed enormously to the book's popularity.

So, too, did the final section, written after Mead had tested her findings in lectures and small discussion groups across the country. Entitled "Our Educational Problems in the Light of Samoan Contrasts" and "Education for Choice," these concluding chapters set the pattern for all of Mead's future work by relating her experience among primitive cultures to the problems of contemporary American society. Mead described several basic differences in how the two societies raised their children; for example, that critical life experiences, such as childbirth, sexual encounters, and even death, are treated as "natural" events by the Samoans, but are concealed from the typical American child. Samoans display little specialization of feeling, particularly about sexual matters, resulting in less marital bickering, frigidity, and impotence among them than among Americans. Even in their work-and-play relationships, Samoans place high value on giving worthwhile tasks, such as caring for infants, to very young boys and girls, with the result that Samoan children see themselves as part of a community that includes their elders. By contrast, American children have no "real" work, only schoolwork and play, a situation that helps drive them from their elders. In addition, Mead found four main differences between the two cultures. First, in Samoa, the stakes are simply not as high as in American society. A child who is unhappy at home need only move to a relative's house for a kind of cooling-off period—an unthinkable solution for an American child. Second, she noted a lack of deep feeling among the Samoans, a casual attitude toward life, that would simply be considered un-American. Third, she noted that the homogeneity of the culture and the lack of choice removed many conflicts from Samoan society that American children could not so easily dismiss, perhaps explaining the greater degree of neurosis among American children than among the Samoans. Finally, she distinguished the large, all-encompassing Samoan family, which in reality took in the whole village, from the tiny, undifferentiated nuclear family that provided the model for American society and which Mead found wanting.

From this analysis Mead drew several lessons for her countrymen, the prime one of which was "that adolescence is not necessarily a time of stress and strain, but that cultural conditions make it so." The stress in our society, Mead said, comes not from any physical passage that children make, but from their "maneuverings" and growing up in our civilization. The solution to overcoming the problems of contemporary American children, she concluded, was not to turn them into Samoans, but to help them prepare for the future, by supplying them with techniques and methods of education geared toward opening the range of choices. "The children must be taught how to think, not what to think," said Mead, a thought that, more than fifty years later, still rings true.

The Samoan expedition set the pace for Mead's voyages among primitive peoples. From the somewhat hesitating, unworldly young woman of twenty-five who went to Samoa, she had been transformed into a knowledgeable, experienced field anthropologist, one of the best in the world, in less than a year. She had mastered the skills of life in the field—observing ceremonies and patterns of behavior, typing her notes and carefully filing them so that her research would not be lost, enduring the hardships of climate and fatigue. More than simply learning technique, she had learned to accept the vagaries of field work and to improvise accordingly, to be constantly prepared for the one ceremony or rite that provides the key to a whole culture—and to recognize the possibility of missing that ceremony. She had learned to be open-ended in her approach to a culture, to throw away preconceived notions about how a primitive people *should* behave—in the mistaken belief that the researcher could thereby "improve" them—and instead to record and observe how they actually behaved, so as to understand them more fully. She had learned, as she once told a young anthropologist who was about to set off on *his* first expedition, that a field worker has to be prepared "to pick up a child that's fallen over, dress a cut on somebody's knee, sit at the bedside of an old man who's having convulsions, or be in the middle of a quarrel where the husband is trying to chop up his wife with an ax." She recognized that each generation of anthropologists—indeed, every field worker—would have to be able to adjust to different and constantly changing conditions and new technology, as she did in later expeditions, when her simple box camera was supplemented by motion-picture film, and, still later, television. Still, it is curious to note that, despite the enormous success that her Samoan chronicle would enjoy, Mead was still apprehensive about presenting the original manuscript to Boas. "I suppose I have betrayed him like all the rest," she thought at the time, fearful that she had "wasted" her opportunity to record a disappearing civilization. Boas, quite wisely, suggested only a few minor changes. Had Mead been supervised by a pedant bent on adhering to "academic standards," *Coming of Age in Samoa* might have been a completely different—and probably ignored—work.

The Samoan voyage assured Mead the opportunity to conduct research where and when she liked, with few of the constraints from Boas and her father that had limited her before. It also led to a change in her personal life: On the ship to Europe, she met a young New Zealand psychologist named Reo Fortune, whom she married as quickly as she could divorce Luther Cressman. Now she set forth with Fortune for New Guinea, then governed by Australia, and the central island of the Great Admiralty archipelago, Manus, where for six months in 1928 and 1929, they settled in a village called Peri.

The Manus culture was built around the acquisition of wealth, measured in the number of dog's teeth accumulated in trade with other villages and surrounding islands. To Mead, the Manus were "a puritanical, materialistic, driving people," not unlike Americans in their fierce devotion to materialism. In the children, the subject of her study, she noted traits similar to their American counterparts. In both cultures, children lacked discipline, showed little or no respect for their elders, and acted as if they were somehow "smarter" than their parents. The Manus adults seemed to care little about enforcing discipline among their young, allowing them for the most part to run free and enjoy their youth. Among American families, Mead noted by way of contrast, the limited amount of discipline was enforced through the withdrawal, either of things—dessert, movies, toys—or of feelings, with the result that there was "little discipline and less dignity." The most striking similarity between the two cultures, Manus and Americans, was their puritanism, with adults in both societies driven by harsh competition, and the children kept separate from the cold, calculated world of their elders.

Her Manus study, *Growing Up in New Guinea*, published in 1930, built on her first book. With the Samoans, Mead confirmed the essential malleability of human nature by showing that adolescent girls from one culture possessed characteristics and patterns quite different from those of another. Depending on their culture, human beings were to some extent pliable, not rigid or one-dimensional.

The Manus experience, however, made her add a codicil to this formula. Human nature is malleable, Mead affirmed; but human malleability has its limits. Observing the Manus child, she saw how he was free to live his life almost in defiance of the harsh life of his parents. But this freedom was only illusory, for as he grew into an adult, the free-spirited Manus boy would become just like his father. As a young man readied to marry and join the society, the Manus boy must earn back from his elders the price they have paid for his bride; thus, he is "shamed" by poverty into assuming the adult pattern of materialistic competitiveness. "It was no use permitting children to develop values different from those of their society," Mead found, for the society would always win. "Human nature is flexible," she concluded, "but it is also elastic—it will tend to return to the form that was impressed on it in earliest years."

The "elastic" effect of culture is very, very strong in a homogeneous culture like Manus. The Manus child becomes the Manus adult because he has virtually no choice but to join the society. In a large, complex, and diverse society like that of the United States, however, the child's options are much greater, and the elastic effect of culture is less strong. Yet in both cultures the emphasis on possessions—dog's teeth among the Manus, money for the Americans—caused Mead to ponder whether there might not be some way to change those values, at least for the Americans, if not for the Manus—to put the emphasis on what a human being is, rather than what he owns.

The conventional wisdom in America, Mead says in the conclusion of *Growing Up in New Guinea*, is that education alone will solve the problem. We put great stock in education—that is, formal schooling—because we have seen the miracle of whole generations of immigrants being remolded into a new crop of Americans. Sometimes we even think that education can create some kind of utopia. But that kind of education is not acculturation, the process by which the beliefs and values of a society are transferred from one generation to the next. That process, for Americans at least, is still tremendously complex and diversified, given the wide range of political, religious, and social thought in America. It cannot be changed simply through the process of education. "All the pleasant optimism of those who believe that hope lies in the future, that the failures of one generation can be recouped in the next, are given the lie," she wrote.

Those who tout education as the universal panacea—and here she was taking a swipe at professional educationists, the kind who perfect "methods of teaching" courses at state teachers' colleges—were perpetuating a sad and possibly harmful myth. Without a change in the values of the wider culture, all the teaching manuals in the world could do nothing to improve children or society. What was the point, Mead asked, of having a well-run, efficient system of education, if the values and substance of the culture are rotten? This overvaluation of education and the concomitant undervaluation of "the iron strength of the cultural walls within which any individual can operate" led to a sad result: "It dooms every child born into American culture to victimization by a hundred self-conscious evangelists who will not pause long enough to build a distinctive culture in which the growing child may develop coherently." Not till Americans realize that "a poor culture will never become rich, though it be filtered through the expert methods of unnumbered pedagogues, and that a rich culture with no system of education at all will leave its children better off than a poor culture with the best system in the world." Throwing the gauntlet to American educators—and parents—Mead urged them to give up their faith in the "magic" of education and to turn their attention to changing their values and to "the vital matter of developing individuals, who as adults, can gradually mould our old patterns into new and richer forms."

With her first two expeditions, examining the process of early childhood development in Manus and adolescent behavior in Samoa, Mead began to fill in her answers to basic questions about human nature. After a brief and wholly unpleasant summer in 1930 studying the "Antlers"—really the Omaha tribe of Nebraska, whom she chronicled in *The Changing Culture of an Indian Tribe*, one of her minor works—Mead and Reo Fortune sailed back to New Guinea to take up what she later called "the field work that was to give me a completely new insight into the natur of sex roles in culture" and the ways in which temperament and culture are related. In short, she was expanding her field of inquiry to the adult world, to discover whether certain temperamental characteristics that modern Western cultures assign to each sex—for example, aggressiveness to males and passivity to women—are innate or the products of one's upbringing. In other words, are differences in temperament associated with men and women—so-called masculine and feminine characteristics—due to birth or acculturation? Is the modern Western pattern of assigning sexual roles universal, or is it possible to find in other cultures permutations or perhaps even a complete reversal of these stereotypes?

Mead set out to find the answers. From 1931 to 1933, she and Reo Fortune made what amounted to an extended field trip to three New Guinea cultures—the so-called mountain Arapesh, the river-dwelling Mundugumor, and the lake-dwelling Tchambuli. As Mead herself later admitted, only "an extraordinary concatenation of circumstances" for which "no notions of serendipity [could] provide an explanation" could account for how they came upon these three cultures. For, as she noted in *Sex and Temperament in Three Primitive Societies*, it would be hard to find three societies that illustrate more perfectly the malleability of sexual roles.

The lucky streak started with the Arapesh. The two ethnologists were actually on their way to study a people living on the plain beyond the Torricelli Mountains, when their porters simply stranded them on a mountain top. Ever-resourceful, they decided to study these people, whom Mead dubbed the "mountain" Arapesh to distinguish them from another group on the plains.

Among the Arapesh, both men and women exhibited what to Western eyes would be seen as a passive, or "feminine," temperament. The goal of the society is to make things grow—yams, sago, taro, and, most important, children. The emphasis is on cooperation; hunting is done in groups, and the men tend their sago patches and yam gardens together, working several gardens at a time with different groups of relatives. The task of literally feeding the next generation is one that both sexes undertake cheerfully.

The Arapesh recognized only one taboo: Anything associated with the sexual act or the reproductive functions of women had to be kept isolated from the rest of society. A menstruating woman, for example, could not work in the garden. Otherwise, both sexes devoted themselves to what Mead called "this cherishing adventure" of providing for the young.

Not everyone conformed to the social structure; even the Arapesh had their deviants. But every effort was made to downplay aggression and violence; and when a grievance had to be righted, as in the case of the abduction of a woman by a man from a different village, the avenging party made every attempt to put the blame on chance, or error, or the sorcery of the people of the nearby plains, who could extract magic from the Arapesh's "dirt"—an excretion, or a piece of half-eaten food, or a bit of bark cloth. The mountain people lived in constant fear of the plains people, but their culture could not have functioned without them, for they provided an outlet or explanation for aggressive behavior, which the society would not condone.

The Arapesh proved something of a disappointment for Mead, since they displayed no differences in temperament between men and women, and she had hoped to determine how the sexes learned (through acculturation) to assume different roles. After seven months, she and Fortune had had their fill of the Arapesh and were eager to investigate new cultures. But there was a logistical problem. With so few researchers in the field at the time, the professional ethic among anthropologists forbade duplication of others' work, for fear that yet another valuable culture would disappear without documentation. Mead and Fortune were already working together as a married couple, so the thought of their working with yet another ethnologist was out of the question. This complication narrowed the possibilities in New Guinea, because Richard Thurnwald was already comfortably ensconced among the Banaro on the Keram River, and Gregory Bateson had laid claim to the Iatmul of the middle Sepik River. Other tribes were inaccessible because the couple's goods and equipment had to be moved by boat. The choice was made for them: the Mundugumor, a relatively unknown tribe a half-day's trip up the Yuat River. They knew nothing about them except that these recent cannibals (now supposedly under control of the Australian government) liked buttons. So, stocked with plenty of buttons, they set their course for Kenakatem, the largest Mundugumor village.

Mead describes the almost accidental nature of this discovery in considerable detail in *Sex and Temperament,* and for good reason: The contrast between the Arapesh and the Mundugumor was so striking that her findings seem contrived. "If I had grasped the full implication of my Arapesh results and cast about to find the New Guinea culture that would throw them most into relief, I could not have bettered the choice of Mundugumor," she said. Here were two peoples, scarcely a hundred miles apart, with practically inverted temperaments. Whereas both sexes among the Arapesh displayed nurturing, caring, maternal temperament, both men and women among the Mundugumor exhibited masculine behavior "without any of the softening and mellowing characteristics that we are accustomed to believe are inalienably womanly." Mothers treated their infants harshly, carrying them about in roughly woven baskets, hanging them in the baskets instead of holding them, suckling their babies very rigidly while standing up, and only when the mother determined the appropriate feeding time. Mundugumor women were equally rough and demanding in sex, biting, scratching, tearing ornaments off their lovers. In fact, the Mundugumor showed no comprehension of the possibility of differing temperaments between men and women. The women were just as violent, aggressive, and jealous as the men, although women were acknowledged to be physically weaker than the men.

This remarkable turnabout can be accounted for to some extent by the organization of Mundugumor society, the basic unit of which is called a "rope." A rope may consist of a man, his daughters, his daughters' sons, his daughters' sons' daughters, and so on; or it may consist of a woman, her sons, her son's daughters, her son's daughters' sons, and so on. This family structure creates tremendous tension and conflict with the society, for in order to marry, the young Mundugumor boy must obtain a wife from another rope. This is done by exchanging the daughter in one rope for the daughter in another. The conflict enters when the father, who may have as many as ten wives, decides to exchange one of his daughters for a daughter in another rope, to obtain a young—and preferably virginal—wife. Thus, father and son may find themselves in fierce competition for the same bride. Under such a system, Mead found, it was not uncommon for a man to express anger at his wife's pregnancy, for fear that she might give birth to a boy who might later become the father's rival. Nor was it unusual for fathers to kill their sons at birth for the very same reason. A similar rivalry existed between mother and daughter. As savage as the Mundugumor culture might have seemed to an outsider, however, it provided the perfect complement to the Arapesh in Mead's overall study of sex and temperament.

If the method by which Mead and Fortune discovered the Mundugumor seemed remarkable, their discovery of the third culture on this expedition, the Tchambuli, was equally notable—and the results were nothing short of marvelous. Again the question arose as to where to go next. The local government officer suggested the Washkuks, a sturdy, lovable, untouched mountain people not unlike the Arapesh. But the Washkuks, upon meeting Mead and Fortune, told them that their villages were scattered (they were living in groups of twos and threes), and they didn't really want to be bothered. (Such are the vagaries of life in the field!) So they left these little bearded men and, on the advice of Gregory Bateson, with whom they had been visiting in his Iatmul village on the middle Sepik, decided to try the Tchambuli, a lake-dwelling culture that had been brought under government protection from other headhunters several years before.

Thus it was that early in 1933 Mead and Fortune established their third camp in the village of Kenakatem, on the shores of Lake Tchambuli (now Chambri). Here Mead found what she later termed the "missing link" in her study of sex and temperament, a culture in which men and women not only differed dramatically in temperament, but were virtually the reverse of what Western society regarded as masculine and feminine in temperament. For here was a culture sharply divided along sex lines, with the men—only recently head-hunters, mind you—spending much of their time in their ceremonial houses, decorating the heads of the victims of some raid on the local bush people—or, more likely, the head of a victim who had been bought from another tribe. Here was a society that, at least on the surface, was based on a patrilineal structure, with precious lands being inherited through the male ancestral lines, and with the men theoretically wielding the power over the ceremonial, sexual, and economic structure of the village; but where, in reality, the women held the power. For, while the men spent their days carving, creating quite beautiful works of art, the women of Tchambuli actually glued together the life of the village. It was the women, working in closely linked groups of ten or twenty, who made the mosquito nets that they traded to the middle Sepik tribes for the green snail-shells *(talibun)* and the mother-of-pearl crescent *(kina)*. Although the men theoretically controlled the culture, in fact they were able to display their supremacy only in masked dances, where they could act out their frustration.

From her close observation of these three cultures, plus her previous work among the Samoans and Manus and her thus far brief experience among Bateson's Iatmul, Mead concluded that "human nature is unbelievably malleable, responding accurately and contrastingly to contrasting cultural conditions." Here were three cultures so diverse in temperamental characteristics as arranged by sex as to be almost unbelievable—the Arapesh, where both men and women were cooperative, unaggressive, and responsive to others; the Mundugumor, with both sexes displaying a ruthless, aggressive, nonmaternal temperament; and the Tchambuli, where the women were the dominant, impersonal, managerial types, and the men exhibited the lesser responsibility and greater emotional dependence.

Upon returning from New Guinea, Mead divorced Fortune and, in 1935, married Bateson. (It is clear that Mead and Bateson had fallen in love when all three were sharing the same roof in New Guinea, and it was only a matter of time before Mead would take action.) From 1936 to 1939, Mead and Bateson lived among "his" Iatmul and "their" Bali, the artistically rich Buddhist culture of that mysterious Indonesian island. From all seven cultures, she developed a formulation of the patterns of sex and temperament she had observed, based on their complementary (and contrasting) natures. For example, she contrasted the aggressive masculine behavior of Mundugumor men and women with the "passive feminine" typology represented by Arapesh men and women. Manus men and women (representing a mix of temperaments on the aggressive side) complemented Bali men and women (a similar mix on the passive side). Tchambuli men ("passive feminine") were placed opposite Tchambuli women ("aggressive masculine"), while Iatmul men ("passive masculine") were deemed complementary to Iatmul women ("aggressive feminine"). Thus, concluded Mead, human nature, at least as measured by temperament, was not a monotone or even a spectrum, but a complicated and intricate mosaic of patterns. This led her to state that "many, if not all, of the personality traits which we have called masculine or feminine are as lightly linked to sex as are the clothing, the manners, and the form of head-dress that a society at a given period assigns to either sex."

This conclusion had relevance not only to these primitive cultures, but to our own as well. To Mead, it suggested that there were three courses open to our society. We could require strict regimentation of roles by gender, largely as we have done, with the resulting loss of individuality and happiness for both women *and* men. Or we could take the radical approach, which in more recent times has gained popularity among certain feminists, of blocking out all sexual differences, a path that Mead predicted would lead to a "flattening" or loss of complexity in our society and a stamping out of diversity. Finally, we could increase the number of options for many and divergent temperaments to coexist, with the knowledge that no single pattern is "right" for all humans or for human nature in general. This last course is the one Mead preferred.

The pre-war voyages among her seven primitive Oceanic cultures—the Samoans, the Manus, the Arapesh, the Mundugumor, the Tchambuli, the Iatmul, and the Balinese—can be said to comprise the foundation of Mead's anthropological research and provided the raw material for not only her major popular books, but also her lesser-known works such as *Male and Female, Cooperation and Competition among Primitive Peoples, Continuities in Cultural Evolution,* and *Balinese Character: A Photographic Analysis* (with Gregory Bateson). After the war she managed a number of return visits to Bali and New Guinea (to follow up on her Iatmul research) and a 1966 trip with Rhoda Métraux to Monserrat in the West Indies.

These visits, however, pale in comparison with her experience in returning to Peri village in 1953. In the twenty-five years since she had first walked among them, the Manus of the Admiralty Islands had been transformed from a Stone Age tribe into a 20th-century society. By the time of her fourth and final visit to Peri, in 1975, the archipelago and the eastern half of New Guinea were unified into a new nation, Papua New Guinea.

How it happened is the subject of one of Mead's most seminal works, *New Lives for Old: Cultural Transformation—Manus, 1928–1953.* In it she describes the New Way, a political and cultural movement led by a mysterious and truly charismatic figure named Paliau Moluat. Born around 1910 on the island of Baluan, Paliau was orphaned at age seven and simply drifted from one relative to another, later taking odd jobs as a laborer and cook and eventually becoming a police boy, the term for a native policeman. He took part in a police boy's strike, and during the war was captured by the Japanese and put in charge of organizing several thousand farm laborers on the island of New Britain. For a while after the war he was under suspicion for being a war criminal, but he was able to avoid conviction, although he had to give up his position with the police.

Then, in 1946, he started getting visions, probably as a result of some sort of messianic metamorphosis. At the time, it was thought that Paliau's transformation was the harbinger of a strange phenomenon, unique to primitive areas subjected to rapid and pervasive cultural invasion by more technologically advanced outsiders. Called a "cargo cult," it is a belief that takes hold of a primitive people, often in a kind of frenzy fanned by a prophet or messianic figure. The people come to believe that a great load of white men's goods—the "cargo"—will arrive, and the whites will either disappear or be made into slaves or servants. To get the cargo, however, the people must renounce all worldly possessions, leading to a binge of destructive activity. In reality, of course, the cargo never arrives, nor does the period of fullness and plenty that is supposed to follow. Usually, civil authorities have to step in to return order to what is often a chaotic and dangerous situation.

Paliau, Mead noted, was no cargo cultist, but a new, if somewhat unorthodox political leader to Western eyes. Whereas the cultists looked back at a romanticized version of life before the white man came, Paliau looked ahead to how the New Guinea mainland and the scattered islands of the Bismarck Archipelago could be united and made part of an ever-changing world. He saw how the war had revolutionized his land and his people. In just a few years, a million soldiers had swept over the islands, with their radios and tractors and airplanes and all the latest paraphernalia of Western technology. And they brought with them new attitudes and ideas, particularly the Americans, whose democratic, open style impressed upon the native New Guineans—especially the young men—that it might be possible for them to be free of the Europeans some day.

Paliau seized this opportunity at the flood. He was, in Mead's analysis, the right man for the times. His political movement, the New Way, capitalized on the rapid technological and cultural transformation that was in the air. Paliau saw that it must rest on three strong legs: First, the traditional schism between the various groups of New Guineans—the lagoon-dwelling Manus, the small-island Matankor, and the inland Usiai—had to be erased. Next, the change had to be complete and rapid. Every aspect of the society had to be evaluated, and those pieces that did not fit into the new plan had to be sacrificed. Scarification, the wearing of grass skirts, and weighting the ear lobes with dog's teeth and shells were to be eliminated. Finally, he saw the need for long-range planning, particularly for the accumulation of capital so that the needs of future generations could be accommodated; in Paliau's words, the New Guineans needed to build "a new chair for our children to sit down on."

It was a bold, almost apocalyptic plan whose very scope nearly led to its downfall. So enthralled were certain elements of New Guinea society with the idea of a cargo cult that one *did* develop, and Paliau had to wait until it had subsided before he could start to put his plan into action. Within months, he built housing, set up a fund for the care of widows and orphans, put aside lands for public works, and established a treasury. The New Way also changed the people's way of life: The Manus were invited to move from the lagoons to the shore, individuals were made responsible for their own economic futures, and the traditional ties with the Catholic mission were broken down. "By 1949," Mead said in her 1957 Terry Lectures at Yale (the basis for *Continuities in Cultural Evolution*), "he had transformed a Neolithic society into a very crude but systematic version of a mid-twentieth century society."

Toward the end of *New Lives for Old*, Mead set down a kind of credo that sums up her own accomplishments of more than fifty years of field work. It stated, first, what she had learned from her mentor, Franz Boas, that the human race was one; that the "races" of mankind were specializations, but they carried with them no measurable differences in their capacity to learn, grow, develop, or improve; that each people possessed a "culture"—a shared, learned way of life—that must be respected by others; and, finally, that although a culture was learned, merely because it was learned did not mean that there were *not* very great differences between cultures—differences, Mead said, that deserved respect, even as it was necessary for cultures to change (and sometimes to be transformed overnight, as the Manus had done) in order to survive and prosper.

These simple concepts became the credo upon which Mead based her later work. They provided the firm ground on which her thoughts on such varied topics as women's liberation, the generation gap, genetic engineering, and the demands of the Third World would be built. It is impossible to understand the later, "activist" Margaret Mead without recognizing that she was, first and foremost, a student of human nature, and that these early expeditions provided her with the body of knowledge necessary to assume the much different, but equally interesting and important, role she would play in the second half of her life.

3
The American National Character

World War II put Margaret Mead and the other three hundred or so American anthropologists in a bind. The war meant that virtually all field work, particularly in the more remote parts of the globe, would have to be abandoned for the duration. For Mead, any possibility of continuing her work in the South Seas was ruled out by the Japanese navy's domination of the Pacific.

But neither Mead nor the rest of her colleagues stood idly by while the war swept around them. Almost all joined the war effort in one capacity or other. Several, including Mead, her husband Gregory Bateson, the psychologist Erik Erikson, and Lawrence Frank of Yale, served on the Committee for National Morale. Mead herself went to work on the government's Committee on Food Habits, and after America's entry into the war she traveled to Britain, where she lectured and appeared on radio to discuss matters of common interest to the Allies.

The question among anthropologists was how to use their special training and knowledge. From Mead's perspective, cultural anthropologists possessed two unique qualifications: They knew how to examine whole societies, and they knew how to study *living* humans, from birth, through adulthood, to old age and death. The notion took hold that perhaps these twin capacities could be put to work in some special way to help win the war.

Out of that sense of mission came a new branch of anthropology, the study of national character. The term "national character" came to have a specific meaning as an area of intellectual pursuit. It derives from the cultural anthropologist's view of the "psychic unity of mankind" which states that, while all humans possess the same innate potentialities for development, no matter what their race, color, language, or nationality, the various cultural backgrounds of peoples influence them and differentiate one people from another. This is the very basis of ethnology: One's culture influences one's development. For example, the Arapesh method of child rearing transmits different cultural messages to the growing child from those that Mundugumor parents transmit to their children; thus, the warm, nurturing relationship of the Arapesh mother toward her child transmits signals to the infant about the Arapesh attitude toward life, a message that is much different from the harsh, rigid child-rearing practice of the Mundugumor mother. This is but a simple example of the acculturation process, of course, but it illustrates the process by which an Arapesh infant becomes an Arapesh adult and a Mundugumor infant, a Mundugumor adult.

National character studies diverted the cultural anthropologist slightly from his accustomed path. Instead of examining small, isolated, primitive cultures, the anthropologist looked at large, complex societies to determine their special cultural patterns. Moreover, national character studies, as the name implies, focused on people as members of nation-states, as, for example, the people of Germany, Romania, Japan, or Britain.

What did Mead and her colleagues hope to accomplish through these studies? Their first thought was to see if studies of national character, coupled with information from other fields, such as public-opinion polling and historical analysis, could shed light on (or, better still, predict) the probable behavior of our allies, our enemies, and even our own people. What did the sneak attack upon Pearl Harbor have to say about the Japanese national character—and what did it predict for future dealings with the Japanese? What, for example, might a study of national character reveal about the Japanese attitude toward surrender? As to the Germans, what could national character studies reveal about how they would respond to postwar occupation and reconstruction, in light of Nazi indoctrination? What could national character studies predict about how the British would get along with the Americans, particularly after the GIs started flooding into the British Isles by the thousands? Would Tommy learn to work with GI Joe? Or would differences in their national characters divide them and impede the war effort? How would Americans, so used to abundant food supplies, react to rationing?

Of course, the study of national character did not spring full-grown from the heads of anthropologists simply because the world was at war, although the war did lend it impetus. Beginning in the late 1920s, shortly after Mead embarked upon her own South Seas studies, anthropology started moving into a new area, no longer confining itself to cataloguing cultural artifacts, ceremonies, and kinship systems, but integrating anthropology with the emerging science of psychology. A new branch of anthropology, the study of culture and personality, began to take shape. It could be traced back to Lawrence K. Frank's work, in 1928 and 1929, with the Social Science Research Council Symposiums on Culture and Personality, to the 1932 Yale Seminar led by Edward Sapir and John Dollard, and to the establishment in 1940 of the Council on Intercultural Relations (later the Institute for Intercultural Studies) by Ruth Benedict. Numerous other antecedents, going back as far as Bronislaw Malinowski's work, took in a wide range of anthropologists, social scientists, and psychologists: Jean Piaget, Carl Gustav Jung, Émile Durkheim, A. R. Radcliffe-Brown, Lloyd Warner, the Lynds, Ruth Benedict, Gregory Bateson, Geoffrey Gorer, and Nathan Leites. (In England, Henry Dicks independently carried on national character studies during the war.) The idea behind culture and personality studies was to link psychology with the way children learn their culture, to attempt to understand how the cultural frame works. This does not mean, of course, that adult personality is determined by early childhood experience; rather, it is a kind of circular system, in which the child is influenced by his culture and he, in turn, may have an effect on his society.

The study of national character took the concept of culture and personality one step further and applied it to the members of sovereign political states. Through interviews with living subjects, analyses of books, films, posters, diaries, letters, and other documents, and, where possible, field work in the subject nation, a composite of the underlying character of a national group could be drawn. When it was impossible to enter the country under scrutiny (as it was in the case of Germany and Japan during the war, and Soviet Russia after), interviews with recent emigrants were substituted. This kind of research became known as "the study of culture at a distance." *

The studies varied in both usefulness and the actual extent of their application. One way in which they were helpful was in giving military strategists some idea of the fighting styles of enemies and allies. The Germans, it was found, pressed their advantage most when they were winning. The British, on the other hand, fought best with their backs to the wall. The Russians attacked only from strength and retreated whenever necessary without losing face. At a completely different level, the studies showed how to change the eating patterns of Americans so as to provide a healthy diet even with wartime shortages. As Mead pointed out, this became a regional problem. People in the North and West gave food moralistic overtones: "Eat your spinach," children were told; "it's good for you." In the South, however, food was looked upon as a commodity that established a pleasure-giving relationship between the giver (the mother or the wife) and the receiver (the child or the husband). When dieticians raised or trained in the North were sent to the South to improve the eating habits of the sharecroppers, they met with a wall of opposition.

One of the more successful national character studies in helping to determine policy was Geoffrey Gorer's work on the Japanese. Gorer found Japanese culture full of dichotomies. The men, for example, were made to feel subservient to their fathers and elder brothers, while behaving aggressively and domineeringly toward women, the latter forced to plead and cajole to get their way. In their early dealings with the Western countries, the Japanese assumed a subservient, or feminine, role toward the bigger and stronger nations. But with their

---

* Mead's postwar work on the study of culture at a distance was devoted primarily to supervising, commenting upon, and editing the work of others, notably that of Geoffrey Gorer, Rhoda Métraux, Martha Wolfenstein, Natalie F. Joffe, Nicolas Calas, and Jane Belo. With Rhoda Métraux she wrote *Themes in French Culture: Preface to a Study of French Community* (1954) and edited *The Study of Culture at a Distance* (1953), outlining the theoretical aspects of the studies begun in 1947 by Ruth Benedict at Columbia University, in what was known as the Research in Contemporary Cultures project. From 1948 to 1950 Mead directed a program at the American Museum of Natural History called Studies in Soviet Culture. This resulted in the 1951 publication of *Soviet Attitudes Toward Authority,* in which she brought together the work of a number of colleagues, notably Gorer, Nathan Leites, and the historian Philip E. Mosely.

defeat of the Russians in 1905, the Japanese attitude toward the West changed, as they now saw the West as weak and feminine. This cultural transformation reached a climax in the invasion of Manchuria, when the Western nations pleaded with but refused to take direct action against Japan, encouraging the Japanese to engage in even more ruthless aggression. Later in the war, when Manila was declared an open city in the hope of protecting it from undue devastation, the Japanese interpreted the move as a sign of weakness and bombed the city with a vengeance, singling out religious and symbolic buildings for devastation.* But Gorer's most perceptive analysis of Japanese national character, according to Mead, was his keen understanding of the role of the emperor. It was Gorer who, in an unpublished paper given at Yale's Institute of Human Relations in 1941, counseled against personal attacks on the mikado. This recommendation, later accepted by the Allied Command in the Pacific, permitted the absolute surrender of the Japanese. Had Gorer's advice not been followed, the war in the Pacific might have been even more protracted.

Few other national character studies had such dramatic results; politics often got in the way. After the war, for example, anthropologists were invited to make recommendations on a program designed to feed large populations in Africa by moving tribes to areas where they could cultivate ground nuts (peanuts). The anthropologists proposed that the participating tribes be subjected to national character studies, in the hope that certain tribes would be found to be more amenable to migration than others. They would pioneer the program, smoothing the way for others whose characters were less conducive to sudden uprooting. The anthropologists' recommendations were ignored, Mead noted, and tribes were thrown into the program willy-nilly, dooming it to failure. Anthropologists were also unable to convince policy-makers to follow two major recommendations concerning postwar Germany: to install a seasoned, mature army of occupation that would provide a strong, fatherly image of democracy, and to allow the Germans themselves to try their war criminals. For a

---

*The sneak attack on Pearl Harbor is an excellent indication of our misreading of Japanese national character. The Americans, who place a high value on life, assumed that the Japanese would not send fighter planes into combat beyond a range that would allow the pilots to return to their bases. As the suicide missions later in the war made clear, the Japanese placed a different value on lives lost in the battle.

number of political reasons, the Allies put in young, inexperienced troops to occupy Germany, and of course tried the Nazi war criminals at Nuremberg. From an anthropological point of view, Mead implied, these were the wrong decisions.

Mead's part in these wartime studies centered on Anglo-American relations. Lecturing before British audiences and talking on the BBC, she tried to explain the differences in national character between the two peoples in an effort to increase their understanding of each other. A constant source of irritation, for example, was the term "partnership." To the British, partnership connoted an equal sharing of a burden, with each partner helping his colleague through the rough spots and downplaying any differences in performance, as if they were playing on the same doubles team in tennis. The Americans thought of a partnership as a business relationship, with one partner supplying the money and the other, the know-how, but not necessarily on equal terms. This invariably led to the British accusing the Americans of trying to take too much credit, whereas the Americans could not understand why the British complained so much.

The presence of so many American troops in Britain during the war also led to conflict over their relations with the native female population. In the United States, Mead explained to her British audiences, a young man could make bold displays of affection, knowing that girls are taught to veto such initiatives. In Britain, however, a girl is expected to be shy and modest but to yield to the demands of a determined suitor—who has been trained to keep *his* demands in check. The lack of clear definition of intent gave rise to numerous embarrassing instances, as when an American boy would ask an English girl for a "date" (a concept totally alien to the British), only to have the girl consider this tantamount to a marriage proposal.

These were by no means the only areas of difference in national character dividing the Americans and the British that Mead discovered. The British thought they had achieved a successful compromise if they had won 95% of their demands; the Americans would say that someone had cheated them on 5% of the deal. Americans tend to organize things on a single scale. They might ask, "What's your favorite color?" whereas the British look at such things in a more complex way: "Favorite color of what? A dress? A flower?" Mead noticed, too, that Americans like to quantify items ("How big is your

town?" or "How many planes did this factory produce last month?"),
while the British blush at such queries for fear of seeming boastful.
Finally, Mead pointed out the differing world perspectives between
the two national characters, the Americans seeing the world as
malleable ("If it's not right, tear it down and build it again"),
compared to the British sense of the world as a delicate, finite plot
requiring husbandry, where man and nature work together.

In 1942, Mead published the first book-length study of national
character, in which she sought to interpret the American national
character not only for America's allies, but for Americans themselves.
The book was called *And Keep Your Powder Dry: An Anthropologist Looks
at America*. The title supposedly comes from Oliver Cromwell: "Trust
God, and keep your powder dry." * She wrote it, she said, to see how
her experience with seven South Seas cultures might shed light on the
strengths and weaknesses of the American character, with the ultimate
goal of helping to win the war. By applying to her own country the
techniques of culture and personality studies used in her Oceanic
work, Mead hoped to find what made Americans tick.

The basis of national character studies, as we have seen, is the
anthropologist's contention that culture shapes behavior and that
cultural influences can be evaluated at the level of the nation-state.
This technique was particularly applicable to the United States, Mead
said, because American culture was formed from a mix of foreign
cultures. Mead characterized Americans as being "third-generation."
In a society formed by immigration, as in the case of the United
States, the first generation carries over some of the culture of the old
country and maintains a sentimental attachment to the fatherland; the
second generation bitterly rejects the old ways, in a desperate attempt
to internalize the new culture, in this case to be "American." For the
third generation, however, the loss of the old culture has not been
filled by any new personality change, as it was for the second
generation of immigrants. The third generation already considers itself
American, but attempts to model itself after some ideal American,
Washington or Lincoln, who of course is not a relative, but is treated
as if he were one's first-generation forebear. As a result, all Americans

---

* *Bartlett's* attributes the quotation to Valentine Blacker, 1778–1823: "Put your trust in
God, my boys, and keep your powder dry!" in Hayes, *Ballads of Ireland, Col. Oliver's
Advice*.

become third-generation. Whereas in Europe the long chain of family history established a continuity of culture for the developing child, in America the sudden coming together of millions of immigrants in a vastly new and different society meant that the developing child had to learn to adjust to change. This is what made America unique.

This "third-generation" quality also helped explain certain American peculiarities, among them the fascination with one's home town. Unlike a European, who can trace his family's history back hundreds of years to the same village, city, or province, an American is without deep roots. Because Americans are constantly on the move and adjusting to changing situations (as opposed to the stability of life characteristic of most European cultures), they sense a void. To fill the gap, an American attaches what seems to a foreigner undue sentimentality to his home town. One American will meet another traveling abroad, and as soon as they establish that they both grew up in Lubbock or Oshkosh (or merely had relatives who once lived there), they become fast and binding friends, at least until journey's end. Such an experience is incomprehensible to a European, Mead noted. It explains in part an American's penchant for joining clubs, groups, and associations, as if becoming an Elk or an Odd Fellow will somehow fill a gap in his life.

And Keep Your Powder Dry also had some important things to say about the American family and its role in cultivating the American national character. Here again, the comparison with Europe is instructive. In Europe, where rigid class structure and firm societal bounds limit upward mobility, the parents' job is to help the child to maintain status in society. Competition among brothers and sisters actually occurs within the family, one child trying to best his siblings. By contrast, American society is virtually without class structure; everyone claims to be "middle-class." Within such a liquid society, parents cannot guarantee their children a place in the order of things. The result is that American parents see their role not as one of *maintaining* status for their children, but of urging the children on to greater success. The child must surpass his parents by forging a new and different—and preferably "better"—future for himself. To do so, he must engage in an almost endless competition, not necessarily with his siblings, as might be the case in European families, but with his schoolmates, playing companions, relatives of the same age, and perhaps his next oldest sibling. The American child is taught to please his parents by competing with his contemporaries for favor. "Be a good boy like Billy," Johnny's mother tells him. "Why can't you get good grades like Elizabeth?" reproaches Mary's father. This competition need not occur within the family; most likely it occurs in the schoolroom or on the athletic field, away from home, with a child seeking parental approval based on his relative success against children from other families.

Instead of a class structure, according to Mead, America has a pecking order. Success is measured on a comparative basis, with those children who surpass their parents in achievement gaining higher status than those who merely maintain their parents' standing. Thus, the child born with a silver spoon in his mouth who as an adult keeps the family business in the black is viewed in American society with less respect than the child from humble origins who as an adult starts his own business. For Americans, Mead noted, success is relative: Where did you start, and how far have you come? The epitome is to be born in a log cabin and grow up to be president.

This pattern of child rearing also relates closely to American attitudes on aggression. Naturally, the question of aggression was prominent in the minds of social scientists at the time Mead was writing *And Keep Your Powder Dry*. As an anthropologist, Mead was aware that culture shapes patterns of aggression. In *And Keep Your Powder Dry*, Mead attempted to offer some insight as to how the culture shaped American attitudes toward aggression and to answer some related questions: Could America hope to win without more lust for battle? Must Americans be as aggressive as their enemies? Finally and simply, were Americans aggressive enough to win the war?

The American child, as Mead's analysis made clear, is encouraged to win his parents' love by competing with his peers, siblings, and companions for achievement in the world outside the home. Unlike their European counterparts, who customarily have a nurse or aunt raise their children for them, Americans raise their own children, including disciplining them. Thus, American parents hold themselves up as models of virtue against which the children can measure themselves. In American homes, the person with responsibility for moral leadership is the mother, or, occasionally, another female—usually an elder sister. Children, and in particular boys, learn how to deal with aggression from women (who are opposed to aggression). The lesson they learn is quite similar to the British pattern of "fair play": Someone else must start the fight, and the opponent must seem to be stronger or have an advantage at the start. But there are a couple of differences, too, for unlike the British, who fight best with their backs to the wall, Americans fight best when they score a victory or two. And while a British child can afford to fight by the rules because his society is relatively homogeneous and everyone abides by the rules, an American child is never quite sure that his opponent does not come from an immigrant group or from some other region that either ignores the rules or fights by different ones. The question of aggression, therefore, is not "Are Americans aggressive enough?" but "Under what circumstances is aggression justified? And against whom?"

Thus, the American pattern of aggression is one in which the child will attack only if provoked or if he remains otherwise blameless. He is encouraged, as part of the whole cultural pattern of succeeding in outside competition so as to surpass his parents, to stick up for his rights; at the same time, though, he is warned (usually by his mother, the family arbiter of morality) against being a bully. To Mead, this explained the familiar image of the American as having a chip on his shoulder, never directly asking for a fight but ever ready to finish one. It explains not only why Americans hesitate to provoke a fight, but also why they must be sure the fight is morally justified.

The American pattern of dealing with aggression also explains why Americans boast so about their accomplishments. In this case, said Mead, an understanding of Anglo-American differences in national character helps clear things up. In the typical British family, for example, table conversation is monopolized by the father. He delivers his version of the day's events to the children, and they listen meekly and obediently. In American homes, the direction of conversation is reversed, with the children being encouraged to chronicle their daily exploits. Sometimes in an effort to impress the parents, however, an American child will embellish the story a little; thus, boasting becomes a kind of release valve for the child to show how readily he is prepared to "stick up for himself" even though aggressive behavior is not overtly condoned by his mother. In later life, then, this characteristic of the American's behavior becomes his way of compensating for his lack of confidence in handling situations where aggression is threatened. During the war, the British, especially the Scots, couldn't stand it. "Americans talk about how much they're going to do," they would say. "We *do* it." For their part, the Americans interpreted the Britons' self-confidence as arrogance. In Mead's interpretation both the Americans and the British were displaying national character traits reflecting their cultural values and upbringing. In her lectures and appearances in Britain during the war, she suggested the use of the terms "overstatement" and "understatement" to replace "boastful" and "arrogant" and thereby the avoidance of unnecessary arguments as to which of the Allies was doing more to win the war.

It was clear to Mead, therefore, that judging by the Americans' peculiar national character, they were fully prepared to do their part in the war. Yet one other question intrigued her: Assuming that the Allies would win the war, would Americans, given their national character, play their part in rebuilding the world? Would they follow the example of the previous generation of Americans who fought a war to make the world safe for democracy and then wrapped themselves in a cocoon of isolationism? Or would they try to build the world anew?

Here again, an examination of American national character gave Mead a special insight. The striving for success that marks the American character is partly accountable to a belief in the Puritan ethic—that hard work, put to proper ends, will be rewarded and, conversely, that failure signals a lack of virtue and efficiency. (In the context of such an ethic, the Depression might have been an indication to the Lost Generation of their failure to take responsible action on an international scale after World War I.) But even a catastrophe as great as the Depression is not enough to stifle American initiative. While Europeans might be content to suffer their lot in life, happy to receive any fate that befalls them, Americans strive to tackle problems. No job is too big for American imagination, intelligence, and inventiveness. The Puritan ethic provides a link between what one does and what one gets as a result. "On it is based our acceptance of men for what they have become rather than for what they were born," said Mead in *And Keep Your Powder Dry.* "On it is based our faith that simple people, people like ourselves, are worthy of a hearing in the halls of the great. On it is based our special brand of democracy."

This aspect of the American national character—the belief that, if you don't like things the way they are, you fix them—was the very quality that Mead thought would propel the nation into the forefront of the postwar reconstruction. Americans built their own culture from what they learned from their native societies, fitting them to their own particular needs. Americans took the skills of the Old World, learned from those who had practiced them for centuries, and adapted them to a new land and a new culture. They did not merely imitate the products of the Europeans in order to produce replicas of their work; instead, they studied how the masters did their work, then adapted their methods to the American system. Americans, she said, learned from the weaver, not the cloth, and American flexibility, this ability to find new solutions to old problems, combined with this skill at adapting the proven methods of the past to the new problems of today, would serve Americans well in their efforts to find a new beginning after the war. In building the world anew, said Mead, Americans must learn what other nations and cultures could bring to the job of world-building and then apply America's special gifts of flexibility and adaptability to the job. For it is their "peculiar blend of moral purpose and practical inventiveness" that sets Americans apart—faith and science in one national character: "Trust God, and keep your powder dry."

4
The American Family

Of all her intellectual pursuits, none would prove more rewarding to Mead than her work on the family, "the institution to which we owe our humanity," as she called it. Although she did branch out into other areas of research (to which the subsequent chapters in this book bear testimony), the family was the subject to which she always returned. And a fortuitous choice of subject it was for her. As a female anthropologist she was able to witness ceremonies and events that were proscribed to her male counterparts; and as a woman, she was able to experience firsthand those events at the core of family life—the birth of a child, its growth and development, and the full turn of the wheel when that child herself becomes a parent. It was a wise choice, too, because Mead's special gift, apart from her capacity for field work, was her ability to assimilate complex information, organize it, and make it understandable to the layman.

Looking back at her work on the family from today's perspective, it is possible to discern several major themes and variations. Chief among these was her belief in the strength and durability of the family. The family has been falling apart for centuries, Mead said, yet it "always creeps back." Hitler tried to eradicate the family. The early Bolsheviks hoped to break up the family because they thought it counterproductive to Marxist theory. Even the ancient Incas attempted to destroy the family. Not only did these efforts fail, but there are virtually no examples in history or prehistory (to the extent that anthropologists have been able to discover) where the family unit—a woman, her children, and a male protector—did not exist. "As in our bodies we share humanity," she once wrote, "so also through the family we have a common heritage." The family's role also has remained constant: in the case of infants to nurture them and teach them trust in their elders and the world around them; in the case of very young children, to help them develop independence so as to be able to move about in the world; and, finally, in the case of older children, to teach them to get along with others, so as to be capable of moving into the world as separate and identifiable human beings. That is the fundamental job of families: to transform children from dependent beings into autonomous individuals able to join the culture. It was the immutability of that function that made the family an "intrinsically tough institution," said Mead.

Despite the indestructability of its basic form and function, the family has been constantly buffeted by the winds of change—and it was precisely in describing and interpreting how societal change affected the family that Mead made her mark. As early as 1929, she was worried about the "curiously exposed and insecure position" of the family. In a 1943 essay entitled "The Family in the Future," Mead put the American family under a magnifying glass and found two significant problems afflicting it: first, a surplus of women without a corresponding role for women who could not or would not get married; second, a longer period of maturation (due to the greater complexity of modern life), leading to the greater possibility of couples getting "out of step" with each other. To overcome the latter problem, Mead suggested that marriages begin with "socially sanctioned, childless contracts" until such time as the couple had matured into what she called a "later child-bearing marriage." As for the surplus-female situation, Mead suggested that society find new ways to give greater dignity to unmarried women, such as removing the guilt from sex and opening the door for unwed women to have children.

This essay foreshadowed several of Mead's later themes: the idea of a "trial," or "two-step," marriage; greater autonomy and respect for the woman as an individual; the need for birth control. It was also slightly outrageous: "Guilt-free sex" and motherhood outside mar-riage were not popular concepts in 1943. And it was not without flaws. For instance, Mead's solution to yet another family problem, that of the child whose temperament did not fit his parents', was to find a foster parent of the same temperament as the child's—a solution which, if implemented, would result in millions of children and parents scurrying around the countryside, all trying to find the right match. More important, though, this essay became the model for a number of similar efforts by Mead. Once every few years without fail, Mead would churn out her "What's wrong with the American family?" essay, in which she would analyze the family in light of changing social conditions. If she had been alive in 1980, she would probably have been writing something about the effect of the punk movement on the family.

In 1947, for example, she took up the war's effect on the family. In an address to the National Conference of Social Work, Mead made one of her earliest and strongest statements on the erosion of the three- or four-generation extended family and its replacement by the nuclear family, consisting of the mother, the father, and their children. Her criticism of the small, isolated nuclear family was to continue unabated for another thirty years. Although the nuclear family did not derive its name from the Bomb, she once said, it is "just about as dangerous as the Bomb." The change meant that all the old support mechanisms that had helped families face hard times, unemployment, family crises, and the day-to-day chore of keeping house and raising children, were taken away. The greatest loss, according to Mead, was taking grandmother out of the home. Suddenly, she said, "women can no longer stand having another grown woman in the house." Now, in the postwar era, young, inexperienced mothers were being asked to take upon themselves all the tasks that a small army helped with in the past.

In addition to the pressure of overwork caused by the new form of family life, the postwar housewife confronted a new and frightening prospect: divorce. Marriage now was considered terminable. As a result, said Mead, the family had become "a ship which may be wrecked by any turn of the tide." Such a condition made the wife's status "exceedingly insecure." She had to prove herself worthy every day: "If she lets herself go, if she gains two more pounds, if she does not keep her stocking seams straight, she will lose her husband." Robbed of her dignity and status, the American wife had to resign herself to being "just a homemaker." Worse still, she found herself being measured against the impossibly high demands established by newspaper advertising and the broadcast media. The only way to avoid the rocky shoals of divorce was for the whole family, especially the husband and wife, to steer the ship of matrimony carefully, "vigilantly tacking, trimming their sails, resetting their course, bailing in storms." With demands like these being imposed on the nuclear family, Mead concluded, "it is incredible that so many families have stayed together."

A few years later, she found a new threat to the American family: urbanization. By the early 1950s, the nuclear family was more isolated than ever before. Cast off in a sea of crabgrass or huddled in a tiny apartment somewhere in the urban wilderness, the young couple could no longer rely on the extended family to help them get started; the tradition of passing property, lands, and dowries from the old generation to the new had vanished long ago. Now the only thing a family could give its children was an education and, if they were lucky, a small down payment on a house in the suburbs. Marriage was no longer based on secure past relationships between the two families, but on the *future*. The young woman looked at her prospective husband and sighed, "He doesn't have anything, except prospects," and the young man looked at her and hoped, "She can't cook, but she'll learn!"

At about this time, too, Mead chronicled yet another breakthrough in American family life, "the most important invention that has been made in the family for a very long time." With Grandma banished from the household, the young American homemaker quickly found herself in need of help to take care of her children. The solution was something called the sitter. Nowadays, of course, the babysitter is commonplace, but in the early 1950s it was a relatively recent phenomenon and one with enormous consequences for the family. For one thing, it gave the child (again for the first time in American culture) a choice of whom to have around the house. When the extended family was still around, the child had no choice; now he did. And, curiously, the institution of the sitter had another, unexpected result: It brought grandparents back into the home, on an intermittent basis at least. Grandma was allowed back into the house, not as a member of the family, but as the sitter. It may not have been her first choice, but at least Grandma (and Grandpa, too) could now have some time with the grandchildren.

Mead's next major commentary on the family had to do with its size. During the war she had come out for larger middle-class families to balance the growth in lower-class families—a kind of social Darwinism. But by the mid-1950s and 1960s, the American family had grown too big, she said. It was true that early marriages with lots of children had given the family "harbors of intimacy and warmth in a world filled with thermonuclear threats of dissolution." But these personal gratifications had to be weighed against the danger of overpopulation. Even though the United States contributed only minimally to the world's population growth, Americans had a grave obligation to the rest of the world to set the pace in population control because Americans consumed 40% of the world's resources. Americans must be the first to limit large families, Mead told her *Redbook* readers, in order to help lay a new emphasis not on the quantity of children, but on the quality of childhood.

Toward the end of her life, Mead found even greater cause for concern regarding the family. By the late 1970s, the list of pathological symptoms had grown: a rising divorce rate; an increase in the number of working mothers, many of them the sole support of their families; more child abuse, and more suicide, alcoholism, and drug addiction among teenagers. The alleged causes of this disarray were also numerous, ranging from parental permissiveness to women's liberation. The situation was more complex than ever; and well-meaning but shortsighted attempts to solve the problem through one-shot attacks (more day-care centers, more drug-abuse programs, more food stamps) only added to the public's sense of futility. Despite this grim picture, Mead could remain optimistic because she knew from her studies of both primitive and modern cultures that the family always survived, no matter how great the turmoil in society. What disturbed her more than these random symptoms of unrest, however, was the continued isolation of the family. The nuclear family, in Mead's view, posed a frightening paradox; in one respect, it permitted the family members to "create their own world," without interference from others; at the same time, its insular nature shut off the nuclear family from the rest of the world. To sort out this paradox, Mead saw the need to provide a support network for the nuclear family comparable to that once provided by the extended family. Exactly how she proposed to do this is a matter to which we shall return.

Mead's thoughts on the family were shaped not only by scholarly research but by personal experience as well. It is easy to understand her concern about the demise of the extended family, for example, when one recalls the role her parental grandmother played in her own education and personal growth. In like vein, her experience as a mother and grandmother certainly colored her views about the effect of culture on the child.

Mead's only child was born to her and Gregory Bateson late in 1939, after the outbreak of the war. It was by no means a routine birth, for Mead had had numerous miscarriages in the course of her three marriages, and the prospective mother took no chances. The actual circumstances of the birth, told in detail in *Blackberry Winter,* were unremarkable, except that it had to be held up for ten minutes while a friend who was filming the event rushed out to her car for a flashbulb. Mead was quite insistent about having the birth filmed. She was convinced from her studies of children in Oceanic cultures that a baby exhibits certain aspects of temperament right from birth, and she wanted to know as much about her child's temperament as possible. She had also arranged to have a pediatrician present, an unheard of practice at the time. The young doctor, Benjamin Spock (who would go on to worldwide fame as the author of *Baby and Child Care*), managed to find a hospital that would comply with Mead's request that no anesthetic be administered and that she be allowed to nurse the baby on demand. The nursing sisters at New York's French Hospital took it all in stride and so, happily, did the baby, Mary Catherine, known as Cathy.

Mead wanted to provide the kind of environment she believed would work best for raising Cathy, but wartime service quickly began impinging on both her husband and herself, so she eventually moved in with Lawrence and Mary Frank and their children. With the help of a nurse and the nurse's daughter, Mead created her own extended family.

This example would serve her well after the war, when she began to write extensively about the nuclear family. Her first concern was for the wife and mother. Not only was she charged with the traditional task of nurturing the children, but because of the isolation of the family, she had to take on the additional task of enforcing all discipline—a "difficult combination to achieve," in Mead's view. As for the husband and father, his traditional task was to provide the child with the socializing model (as opposed to the biological model provided by the mother). He was the "dynamic contrast," the representative of the outside world into which the child must eventually pass. Within the nuclear family, though, with no other adult males (uncles, grandfathers, cousins) around to help, the postwar father had to fulfill this role alone. Neither mother nor father had an easy job.

Fortunately, Mead was at the ready with some helpful advice to parents. She called for a new ethic for parents, in which both husband and wife would learn to respect each other and yet tolerate differences of opinion on how to raise the children. Addressing the men, Mead said they needed to give their wives the security of knowing they could stand up to them without quarreling and without making the children feel insecure about the stability of their parents' marriage.

As for the qualities she thought most valuable to a parent in helping a child toward maturity, Mead came up with the following credo:

> To treat each child as an individual person; to realize that children are not adjuncts of their parents, but are individuals in their own right.
>
> To set a child's feet on her own path and allow her to follow it; yet to be there when that path seems hard to follow.
>
> To be willing to listen, and listen, and listen.
>
> To be brave enough to show disapproval when one feels that something is wrong, even though by doing so one may be risking rejection by the child.
>
> To stand up for one's own beliefs and so make one's responsibility for a child worth having and keeping.

She was keen, too, on the duty of parents to acquaint children with tragedy and death, facts of life that had all but been washed from the sterile environment of the modern-day home. (This was an old theme of hers, in fact, going back to *Coming of Age in Samoa*, where she praised the relative ease with which Samoan children, exposed to death at an early age, dealt with it compared to their American counterparts.) She encouraged parents to develop a sense of historical perspective and a grasp of language in their children, and to create in the home those conditions necessary for first-rate achievements—a place of quiet contemplation, for example, where children might dream their most vivid dreams and conjure up wonderful and novel ideas. She thought children should be given the opportunity to learn to meet and enjoy people of different ages and interests, but not necessarily of different sex; as a matter of fact, she thought there was too much boy-girl activity; too many junior-high-school children were going steady, and she favored encouraging more same-sex friendships among pre-adolescents.

In an article that summarizes her work on childhood, Mead wrote in 1972 that Western society's effort to understand the nature of childhood and to put that knowledge to work in bringing up children was one of its finest achievements. Every culture since the beginning of time, she wrote, has sought two achievements with regard to its children. The first is to create an image of human nature. For example, the Russians see the child as a rough, strong individual who must be tightly swaddled to prevent him from hurting himself. The French, on the other hand, see the child as a delicate creature who must be loosely wrapped and kept safe. The second point has to do with the culture's image of the relationship between the parents and the child. The English culture, for example, sees the parent as a gardener, cultivating the natural growth of the child. Germans, however, conceive of the child as a flower in a pot, with the parent constantly battling weeds and poor growth, that is, enforcing discipline. The French see the child as a young tree, ready to branch out but also requiring careful pruning.* She was careful to note that it was not the single event or single peculiarity of behavior in raising a child (such as the practice of swaddling), but the whole panoply of techniques and methods, that created a recognizable style of childrearing.

What was most important, said Mead, was the greater understanding of the child brought about by the child-development studies of this century. Far from being what the philosopher William James called a "buzzing confusion," the infant (as these studies showed) possessed a remarkable sense of space, sight, sound, visual patterns, and movement, and was infinitely more complex and capable of learning than

---

*These cross-cultural patterns were first noted by Mead in her work with Martha Wolfenstein on the Columbia University Research in Contemporary Cultures project, which culminated in their co-edited work, *Childhood in Contemporary Cultures*. See bibliography.

was once thought. As a corollary of that finding, said Mead, child development specialists had also come to the understanding that childhood was not a state but a process. Through their studies, these specialists (notably the Swiss, Jean Piaget) had produced a sizable body of evidence to show that the growing child exhibits fairly regular patterns of crawling, walking, and talking, patterns which were *not* greatly affected by differing styles of child rearing from one culture to another. In addition, Freud's work on the impact of childhood on adult life made it clear to Mead that the "continuing interplay" of one's past and present could not be ignored when studying the child.

For Mead, these developments foretold exciting possibilities for future studies. How could these findings be applied to our knowledge of the differing styles societies have adopted to acculturate their young? Take the matter of how different cultures teach the infant and toddler to learn about the world around them. The Chinese allow the child to see but not touch a thousand interesting and stimulating things. The French emphasize the sound of the human voice, so French mothers talk constantly to their children. American children are raised on the theory that physical activity and contact are the way to acquaint the child with the larger world. With so many different cultural styles of child rearing, yet with basically the same potential for individual growth and development no matter what his culture, the child remained a wondrous object of study for Mead throughout her long career.

It would be a serious omission to fail to mention Mead's work on adolescents and grandparents. Her career started with a study of adolescents, but for years after writing *Coming of Age in Samoa* she continued to examine the problems of this age group. The effects of a steadily declining puberty age on social mores, the intricacies of boy-girl relationships (dating, "going steady"), the menace of juvenile delinquency, the question of discipline ("permissiveness," as it was known in the 1950s), the definition of ethical values (everything from premarital sex to the morality of the undergraduate panty raid), the means and methods of the adolescent's education—all these were fair game for Mead. It would be safe to say that she devoted as much or more to her efforts on the study of the adolescent as she did to any other subject.

Her most interesting if not necessarily her most substantive contribution to the study of adolescents, however, was her work on the generation gap. She developed the concept of the generation gap (I'm not sure she coined the phrase, but she was certainly the person most closely identified with it) during the period of student unrest in the late 1960s. The term caught on after students at Columbia University seized the administration building in protest over the construction of a college gymnasium in the Morningside Heights neighborhood surrounding the university. The Columbia upheaval was the first of dozens of such student protests in the United States and reflected growing unrest among young people both in America and abroad. Combined with the burgeoning protest against the military draft and America's involvement in Vietnam, the student revolt seemed to give evidence of a massive, worldwide adolescent rebellion of a kind not witnessed before in history.

As a member of the faculty at Columbia and an alumna of its sister school, Barnard, Mead was perplexed about the student takeover and searched for the basic cause. She laid out her thoughts in a lecture at the American Museum of Natural History, which was later published as *Culture and Commitment: A Study of the Generation Gap*. In this small volume (one of her least compelling works, in my opinion) and in a number of other more cogent essays, she described three kinds of cultures: *postfigurative,* in which children learn primarily from their elders; *cofigurative,* in which both children and adults learn from their peers; and *prefigurative,* in which adults, too, learn from their children. In a postfigurative culture, such as those of the Oceanic societies Mead had studied, change is so slow as to be almost imperceptible, and each generation grows up expecting to repeat the way of life handed down by previous generations. In a cofigurative society, such as that of the Israeli kibbutz, children rely as much on their peers as on their elders for the means of acculturation. The same is true of immigrant societies, such as those in the United States and Canada, where the second and third generations reject the norms of the pioneering generation in favor of their own.

The prefigurative culture is totally new. It is based on the premise that since World War II, cultural change has occurred so much more quickly and in such greater dimension than ever before, that those born before the war simply cannot comprehend it in the way that the postwar generation *must* understand it in order to survive. For the first time in history, the older generation cannot teach the young how to cope with the startling new kinds of changes that are occurring in the world: the threat to life from the bomb; the population explosion, which unless contained could wipe out all of mankind's gains; the deterioration of the environment; the war between the haves and the have-nots, both within countries and between countries; and the information/communication explosion—television, satellites, computers—which simultaneously make matters more complex and easier to understand. "Our small children are standing on the moon looking back at the earth," Mead said, "while the adults are shaking their heads and trying to remember what is in the sky."

This was not simply normal adolescent rebellion or generational conflict, the age-old battle between father and son and between mother and daughter that has fueled the minds of writers for centuries. This was "something very different and far more serious," according to Mead. Nor was it a situation (as the term "generation gap" was popularly misconstrued) of the young saying to their elders, "We are smarter than you." The young have always thought themselves wiser than their elders. What was new was that, for the first time, the young were in a situation that their elders had never faced and therefore could not explain—the possibility of the destruction of the world, on the one hand, and the creation of a totally new, unforeseeable world on the other. The dropping of the bomb made it inconceivable for those who had lived before Hiroshima to teach those born after it how to cope with the speed and dimension of postwar change. "There are no elders who know what those who have been reared [since the war] know about what the next 20 years will be," said Mead. Strictly speaking, the gap was one between eras, prewar and postwar, not between generations. "Generation gap," an unfortunate choice of terms (and one that Mead rescinded, in favor of the less catchy but more accurate term, "era gap"), caused an undue amount of confusion among the public. But the underlying concept, when placed in proper perspective, is sound.

But was it possible to bridge the gap? Yes, said Mead, and grandparents were the link. Grandparents (in fact, all elderly people) were "the best living examples of change." Like her own paternal grandmother, who died in 1928 at the age of eighty-two after witnessing the coming of the horseless carriage, the flying machine, the telephone, the radio, and moving pictures, all grandparents were "living repositories of change." In one of her most exquisite essays (made so, I think, because of her deep and abiding love for her grandmother), the chapter on grandparents in *Family,* Mead describes grandparents as "a refuge and a point of anchorage." They show the whole cycle of life: "Through a grandmother's voice and hands the end of life is known at the beginning." Despite the generation gap, grandparents can still fulfill an ancient function, to teach the young "how the whole of life is lived to its conclusion—in the past by running exactly the same course that one's father had run, and today by a readiness to run each day, each week, each year a new and untried course." Even with the speed and dimension of change in today's world, the experience of grandparents who have faced change themselves can give young people "a special sense of sureness about facing the unknown." She summarized her belief this way: "In the presence of grandparent and grandchild, past and future merge in the present." In a sense, Mead tried to close the generation gap by showing that the future could be faced only when three (or more) generations worked together.

In the course of a half-century of writing about the family, Mead made the case for a number of reforms designed to save this vital institution. As with many of her suggestions for social reform, however, the more specific they were the less feasible they became. For example, she was concerned about the rising divorce rate, particularly among young couples. The greatest enemy of young marriages, she wrote, is "the fact that from the beginning we anticipate their failure." She was an early advocate of predivorce counseling to prepare parents and children for the pain and anxiety of the coming divorce, and she also thought it was wise to develop innovative ways to prepare women for the possibility of divorce, particularly to find ways to overcome the sense of failure brought on by divorce—all perfectly good ideas, within limits. But taking the concept a step further, she proposed that newlyweds purchase "divorce insurance" (she later changed it to "marriage insurance") to provide for the wife and children in the event of divorce. The proposition never caught on, even though it seems to make sense at first glance, because few couples go into marriage expecting to divorce; in fact, taking out insurance in anticipation of divorce is antithetical to the whole concept of marriage. Another of her ideas with no practical basis was her call for the "family impact statement." This was to be a document, analogous to the environmental impact statement, whereby each piece of federal legislation and every federally funded project would be evaluated for its effect on the American family. Once again, the idea sounds plausible, until one considers how much useless paperwork it would generate.

But Mead cannot be entirely faulted for going out on a limb with bold ideas. Her mission was to challenge others with her sometimes zany schemes for social reform. In many cases, though, she offered a sobering word of caution about the fashionable but ill-conceived proposals of others. In the early 1970s, when Congress was playing with instituting a basic child allowance, Mead warned that the program might actually encourage poor families to have children. When feminists were clamoring for the government to provide more money for day-care centers, Mead stated flatly that day care was fine for women who had to support their families, but not as a "national idea." She felt strongly that feminists were putting too much emphasis on creating conditions to "free" mothers to work and not enough on creating conditions to provide children with continuity of care from their mothers. She had strong words, too, for parents who saw day care as the ultimate in child care: "People who want children in order to turn them over to a day-care center," she said, "had better not have them in the first place." This was not the popular image of Margaret Mead speaking here. This was a woman with considerable experience with children, who saw no need to mince words.

Not that Mead was unsympathetic to the very real problems of modern-day parents. She worried especially about what was happening to parents as their children grew up and flew the nest, leaving them to grow old alone. "Motherhood is like being a crack tennis player or ballet dancer—it lasts just so long, then it's over," she once said. This was a problem not to be overlooked, because medical breakthroughs were keeping alive many people who in the past would not have lived and keeping others more vigorous than any oldsters had ever been. She advised older people to take practical steps to break their melancholy, such as moving to a new community, or cultivating the more sophisticated pleasures of life—theater, fine foods, or travel. For the women, she thought it wise to prepare for a second life of work, one not centered on their husbands and children. Yet Mead knew that what old people really wanted was something that they could not get, now that they had been banished from their children's homes: a sense of being cherished for themselves as individuals and for the one thing only grandparents could give children, the "priceless gift of serenity."

Mead was concerned, too, about the rapid and substantive changes in the institution of marriage. Americans have always had a different attitude about marriage and sexual relations from Europeans, she explained. In Europe, marriage was often an arranged affair. The husband usually was considerably older than his wife and took responsibility for initiating her into the ways of sex and domestic life. In contrast, Americans married by choice, married young, and often married strangers. Neither partner really knew that much about the other person or about sex or how to make a marriage work. These conditions made marriage in the United States "a greater gamble than it is in other countries where marriages follow more traditional lines," Mead noted as early as 1929. Yet, particularly after World War II, both partners in the American marriage had high expectations for success, based on "greater frankness, greater articulateness, greater sharing" than ever before. The marriage—and the family—would supply the young couple with all their needs: happiness, independence, togetherness.

Unfortunately, high expectations too often lead to drastic failure, to which the American form of marriage is not immune. The emphasis on couples finding happiness only with themselves ("Now it's couples, couples, couples—Noah's Ark," Mead once complained) meant that any breakdown between the partners could threaten the whole family, as evidenced by the growing divorce rate. Even increased longevity was having an effect on marriage. In bygone days, it was not uncommon for a man to bury two of three wives—not a pleasant occurrence, but one way to keep the marriage fresh. Today, said Mead, "the contemplation of fifty years together makes people less willing to tolerate an unsuccessful marriage." Finally, the tremendous revolution in sexual matters, thanks primarily to the Pill (what Mead termed "as important a change as the discovery of nuclear energy"), relieved married couples of the fear of unwanted births and freed women to become valued as individual people, not just baby makers. Yet with the sexual revolution came some serious problems for young people unprepared to deal with sex that "contains neither love nor delight." The young, supposedly more sophisticated in sexual matters than their elders were at their age, were turning out to be nearly as clumsy and inexperienced by the time they were ready for marriage.

What must be done to prepare young people for the responsibilities of married life and parenthood? Mead toyed with several ideas. In 1963, she proposed that all public schools be required to teach a course on family life: how to take care of babies, budget family finances, and solve typical family-related problems.* Ten years later, she embellished the proposal with a suggestion for "trial parenthood." Couples contemplating marriage would go through a series of real-life tests: babysitting for an infant one night, minding a couple of three-year-old twins for a weekend, taking a whole troop of children to a picnic, and so on. Couples who went through the internship would have a much better idea of whether they wanted to have children.

The proposal that raised the biggest furor, however, was the "two-step marriage." Mead's rationale for creating two kinds of marriage was reasonable enough. She was deeply concerned about the state of marriage in America: young couples marrying too early (many because they had to); having babies right away and quickly running into financial troubles; arguing with each other; divorcing; fighting over custody of the children and child support—a scenario fraught with anguish. Mead hoped to find some new way to put the emphasis back on human relationships in marriage and less on the physiological drive of sex; to perpetuate the idea of marriage as a lifetime commitment; to maintain the principle of marriage as a matter of personal choice, not one forced by one's parents or an unwanted pregnancy; and to make sure that the children of the marriage would be able to maintain a lifelong tie to both parents. While advocating these noble goals, Mead was also abundantly aware that today's young people consider sex to be a "natural activity" that cannot be postponed by any societal constraints. Moreover, the postwar attitude toward marital commitment—that no one should be trapped in an unhappy marriage forever—also had to be taken into account. How, Mead asked, could these conflicting goals and constraints be balanced so as to create a new kind of marriage?

Her answer came in a 1966 *Redbook* column. Marriage would be divided into two kinds: the "individual marriage" and the "parental marriage." In the individual marriage, the couple would be legally married but would agree not to have children; in the case of divorce,

---

*Many schools have instituted such courses, though not necessarily as a requirement. See Robert Cassidy, "Total Training for Parenthood," *Parents Magazine,* September 1973.

neither partner would have any financial obligation to the other. The parental marriage would require a new marriage license and would be more difficult to contract, having to be preceded by a successful individual marriage. It would also be more difficult for a parental couple to break up, and there would be strict rules about the financial support of the children and their continued relationship to *both* parents.

The reaction was immediate—and vociferous. One woman likened Mead's plan to "legalized prostitution," and added, "Sex is not a shoe to be tried on, and if it does not fit, try another." Experts on marital affairs asked how Mead would prevent "individually married" couples from having babies and who would decide when such couples could pass on to parental marriage. Many young people wrote asking Mead, "Why get married? Why not just live together?" She did get some support. One young married woman said she believed some of her contemporaries were adopting Mead's plan on a voluntary basis, postponing having babies until the marriage had proven solid. That's what she and her husband had done, this correspondent told Mead, and it seemed to be working.

On the whole, however, the reaction was overwhelmingly negative. For the first time in her career, Mead had to recant on an idea: "It now seems clear to me that neither elders nor young people want to make a change to two forms of marriage," she said in a follow-up article in *Redbook*. In a tone of disgust, she implied that her critics were content to keep the present system of marriage, even if, in Mead's view, it didn't work. She was especially disappointed in her more youthful detractors, those who favored "living together." Such a position, she said, was nothing more than a demand for a new moral standard that sanctioned premarital sex. Young couples who merely lived together wanted personal commitment without the moral or legal responsibility of marriage; and when they did finally marry in the conventional sense, these same young people expected marriage to fulfill the ideal, to be perfect and forever—a position, she said, that was "hopeless," "ridiculous," and "utterly untenable." She warned couples who lived "outside the law" that they faced "censure, punishment, disgrace and damaged careers" and advised them that if they wanted full-time companionship, to get married, use contraception, and risk divorce later. "You are risking even more if you don't," she scolded, presumably referring to public censure and legal liability.

It's hard to know what to make of Mead's atypical harangue against the young and her bitter response to her critics in general. In one respect, she was right to warn against the legal complications of living together, as the palimony cases of more recent times have indicated, although so far, these suits have been limited to the girlfriends of movie stars, rock musicians, and tennis players. There also seems to be anecdotal evidence to indicate that many couples are waiting a few years for their marriages to solidify before taking the next step to parenthood. But that is somewhat different from Mead's proposal for a two-step marriage, complete with licenses and legal restrictions. Certainly it is the case that many couples are living together outside wedlock and that they consider this a form of trial marriage; and it seems equally true that many of these couples go on to conventional marriages, and that the institution of marriage seems as strong as ever in the United States today. This is not to disparage Mead's proposal, for it was based on sound ideals and noble goals. But for once in her life, Mead's reach exceeded her audience's grasp.

And what of the future of the family? Mead saw the isolation of the nuclear family as the overriding problem. Looking back through the history of America, Mead noted that the pioneering families were cut off from society, too, but they were completely self-sufficient, whereas today's nuclear family is anything but self-sufficient. It consumes more than it produces and, cut off from the rest of society, remains helpless in the face of adversity. What is needed to save the nuclear family, said Mead, is a "community" to surround it and support it, a three-generation community similar to the extended family. This is especially the case for the children, who need people other than their mothers and fathers around to "take up the slack in the relationships with their parents" and to provide additional models of adult behavior and temperament in order to see that "gender is one thing and temperament is another." The boy whose father is fiery and blustery would then be able to look at the serenity in his grandfather's eyes and understand that it is possible for a male to exhibit a wide range of temperamental characteristics and still hold onto his masculinity. Similarly for the young girl whose mother is deferential and submissive to her husband, but whose aunt is aggressive and defiant to her brother-in-law, femininity would be seen as encompassing a broad scale of behavior. In the closed walls of the nuclear family, however, children have only their parents as models of sex and temperament.

Mead sought to end the isolation of the nuclear family by creating something she called "clusters." Clusters were to be composed of one or more nuclear families, surrounded by a larger community—older married couples, childless couples, singles, teenagers from other households, and so on. Each family would maintain its own home, but would somehow—and on this she was vague—have an association with each other. They would *not* be communes: Mead was emphatic on that point. Communes were political experiments. But the cluster would be like a commune in providing an unusual "setting" for the family and in offering a wide variety of people to care for and care about the nuclear family—somewhat reminiscent of "the old neighborhood," that mythical place where old men sat on the stoop and watched over the children on the street; where mothers would share tips about how to get their infants to take a pacifier, as they rocked the baby carriages together at the local park; and where the teenaged boys and their uncles and fathers got together to install new brakes in the neighbor's car. It is a romantic vision of family life and probably an unrealistic one for today's world. Mead suggested that the place to try the idea was in the academic community, but it may be too far-fetched even for the intelligentsia.

The need persists for some form of family "cluster" as described by Mead, but exactly what form this new social structure might take is difficult to discern. In the late 1960s the postwar baby-boom generation tried the commune and found it wanting; perhaps any attempt to revive the extended family would be equally doomed. Somehow, though, there must be a way to combine the benefits of the nuclear family with the advantages of the extended family. Mead sketched a rough outline of the idea. What is needed today is for some enterprising social architect to complete the final drawings and start building the prototype family of tomorrow.

5
The Future of the Schools

"American education is obsolete," Margaret Mead told an interviewer in 1972. "We were pioneers in the public school system, but it's become outdated like British industry. . . . The university system in both Europe and America is 400 years behind the times."

In her usual unrestrained manner, Mead here reveals the substance of her critique of America's schools. Yet until she entered college, her own formal education consisted of two years of kindergarten, one year of half-day school in the fourth grade, and six years of high school. The skimpiness of this curriculum is even more remarkable considering that she came from a family of educators—her father a university professor, her mother a teacher during graduate school, her grandmother at one time a high school principal, and her paternal grandfather a superintendent of schools in Ohio. As she explained it, though, her family didn't approve of schools that kept children chained to their desks all day long instead of being outside doing something.

So young Margaret learned from those around her. Her mother arranged lessons for all the Mead children in such crafts as drawing, carving, painting, modeling, and basketry. She made them play with children of all classes and types to drive bigotry from their minds. Margaret spent most of her time memorizing verse, playing games, making up and performing plays, and reading—sometimes sneaking a few extra minutes of reading time by hiding in the hollow of a tree when she was supposed to be doing something active.

Then there was her grandmother. Besides giving Margaret a one-hour lesson every day, she was constantly showing her new ways to do things, encouraging her to act out a fable, and—because she insisted that every child should live on a farm at some time in his life—teaching the virtues of the agrarian life on the farm in the Buckingham Valley they moved to when Margaret was eleven years old. This tutelage lasted well beyond Margaret's college years. "You are always in the thoughts of grandmother by the sea," her grandmother once wrote her. "P.S. Apartment is spelt with one P." In later life, the lessons learned growing up in what she called a "hotbed of educational discussion" served Mead well in formulating her own thoughts on the process of learning.

It was in the early 1930s that Mead first became identified as an education reformer. Her background clearly suited her for the role. As an anthropologist, she concentrated on young people—the units, as it were, of organized learning. In *Coming of Age in Samoa* and *Growing Up in New Guinea,* she began to draw conclusions about young people's behavior that would have considerable implications for educators. Her published works were also among the first anthropological studies to apply the emerging science of psychology (the field in which Mead had earned her master's degree) to ethnological studies; this application of the social sciences to education was to become the essence of the so-called progressive education movement, which numbered among its leaders Jane Addams and John Dewey.

Mead's formal identification with the progressives came through Lawrence K. Frank. In 1927, Frank and Beardsley Ruml were given a foundation grant to improve nursery school education. They divided their efforts into research on child development, actual training of teachers in this field, and aiding sympathetic groups, such as the American Association of University Women. In 1931, Frank moved over to the General Education Board and set up a similar plan for the study of adolescents. The idea was to bring in experts trained in psychoanalysis, sociology, anthropology, and the science of physical growth, to study the educational problems of this troubled age group. Among those invited to participate were Erik H. Erikson, Robert S. Lynd, W. Lloyd Warner, and Mead.

By the early 1930s, then, Mead found herself part of what G.

Franklin Giddings termed the educational protocracy, the advance guard of a new movement in education. With Lawrence Frank's $2-million grant, they designed an ambitious program of research. Besides studying the physical and emotional growth of adolescents and publishing curricula and books designed specifically for that age group, they mapped out an eight-year study of new education programs in some thirty schools, with a follow-up of graduates of those schools through college. In the summer of 1934 the project also sponsored the Hanover Seminar on Human Relations, whose goal was to develop an outline of all available knowledge about human behavior. Although the "Hanover Outline" itself was never completed, the seminar did lead to the publication of a number of trailblazing books, among them John Dollard's *Criteria for the Life History;* James Plant's *Personality and the Cultural Pattern;* Robert S. Lynd's *Knowledge for What;* W. Lloyd Warner, Robert J. Havighurst, and Martin B. Loeb's *Who Shall Be Educated?;* and Mead's own *Cooperation and Competition Among Primitive Peoples.* In addition, Mead worked on a study of the physical growth of adolescents and served as an adviser to the project's Adolescent Study and as a member of the Committee on the Function of the Social Sciences in Education. If, indeed, there was an educational protocracy in the 1930s, Mead was very much part of it.

Unfortunately, World War II put an end to much of the research, but the movement's leaders also erected their own roadblocks. For all his brilliance in creating the projects, Frank never included representatives of the children or adolescents under study. (Mead would later criticize it as being by professionals, for professionals.) After the war, the progressives, under the banner of the Progressive Education Association, got muddled up with the New Education Fellowship, a radical group that hoped to change society by reforming the schools, using the students as agents of change. It became an easy target for McCarthy-type witchhunters.

But the progressive movement collapsed primarily from the weight of its own expectations. As Mead would later note, everyone associated with the progressive movement assumed that some sort of *product* would evolve from it, a document that would set American education right. Both the Hanover Seminar and the Committee on the Function of the Social Sciences in Education did result in the publication of a number of influential books and studies.* What they all misunderstood at the time, however, was that the progressive movement was a *process* that influenced others and created a legacy that would endure for generations. The progressives changed educators' thinking about adolescent development, making such concepts as the differing states of maturation of adolescents and "differential readiness" (for engaging in social activities) part of the vocabulary of the field. The Eight-Year Study resulted in a softening of the institutional structure of the colleges that participated in it, enough to break the grip of the college entrance examinations on secondary schools, according to Mead. Most important, it created a network of leaders and reformers who believed in spreading the idea of changing the schools. Many of the ideals of the progressive movement would filter down to our present day. The Head Start program of the 1960s, which improved the nutrition and education of preschool children in poor areas, is a manifestation of progressive movement thinking. As Mead noted, the Eight-Year Study came out against the "single ladder" system in use in American schools, whereby only one avenue—the passage from grade to grade, following prescribed courses—is open for the student to be certified with his diploma. More recent commentators, notably Ivan Illich in his *De-Schooling Society,* have argued instead for a "lattice," providing many routes to the same goal. Mead herself was pessimistic in the early days of her anthropological studies about educational reform leading to social change (notably *Growing Up in New Guinea*), but her postwar voyages to the South Seas caused her to modify her pessimism.

Margaret Mead's contribution to education rests equally on her work as a teacher, lecturer, and philosopher of education and on her seminal writings. Of the latter, two essays written during the 1950s— "The School in American Culture" and "Why is Education Obsolete?"—represent the most precise distillation of her thoughts on the

*The committee's publications included: Committee on the Function of Social Studies in General Education of the Commission on Secondary School Curriculum, *The Social Studies in General Education* (New York: Appleton-Century, 1938); Progressive Education Association, *The Study of Adolescents: Commission on Secondary School Curriculum of the Progressive Education Association* (New York: Appleton-Century, 1937–40); *Adventure in American Education,* 5 vols. (New York: Harper, 1942); and *Evaluation of the Eight-Year Study* (Chicago: University of Chicago Press, 1939–40).

76 Margaret Mead

subject. Yoked with several lesser-known but equally significant essays
written during this period, they neatly summarize her educational
philosophy.

"The School in American Culture," originally given as the Inglis
Lecture at Harvard University in March 1950, and later published as
a small book, is remarkable not only because it presaged Mead's own
thinking on the so-called generation gap, but also because it forecasted
the kind of educational reform that would be necessary in the post-
Sputnik era—more than seven years before the Soviet satellite was
launched. Like much of Mead's best work, it is more notable for its
broad analysis of the root causes of problems than for any of its
suggested solutions.

Throughout America's history, Mead said, three images of the
American school have coexisted. The first is the little red schoolhouse,
"the symbol of a stable, democratic, slowly changing, real American
world," ever desirable, but rarely attained in real life. The second is
the academy, where the privileged of society send their children so
that they may be imbued with the values of the past, on the theory
that the institutions and cultural values of the past helped put the
privileged in the relatively comfortable position they enjoy today.
Finally, there is the city school, that rough-and-tumble port of entry
where in the century from 1840 to 1940 the children of immigrants
from Europe and Asia learned not only English and the three R's, but
also how to be an American; today, the same process continues,
although the "immigrants" now hail from Puerto Rico, Mexico, the
West Indies, or even the rural South or Appalachia. These three
images of the school—the idyllic (and, practically speaking, nonexis-
tent) one-room schoolhouse, with its rosy-cheeked schoolmarm dish-
ing out book learning, common sense, and conservative social values
to the impressionable young of America's small towns; the dizzying
heights of the academy, with its own grandiloquent version of Mr.
Chips dispensing culture to the future movers and shakers of society;
and the city school, with its rugged, no-nonsense teacher, herself a
second- or third-generation example of the success that can be
attained with hard work and application to studies, trying to make
good Americans out of the meanest raw material—all three are
present in any discussion of American education: Should the schools
concentrate on useful foreign languages, such as French or Spanish, or
should they require the classics, Latin and Greek? (Why not the ever

more useful Russian and Chinese, for that matter?) Should the schools focus attention on "academic" courses, or should they prepare students for the real-life demands of a job, a home, and other familial and societal obligations? Should academic courses be required, elective, or some combination of each? What about liberal arts versus vocational or professional curricula? Should sex education be made part of the school curriculum and, if so, how should it be taught and at what age levels? These were some of the questions being argued in an endless debate as to whether schools should be oriented toward the past or toward the future.

The division of the American school into the little red schoolhouse, the academy, and the city school can also be viewed from a cross-cultural perspective, Mead said. The kind of nurturant, sympathetic relationship that might be found between the mythical schoolmarm and her innocent young charges in the little red schoolhouse is also found in those societies in which the children are raised by child nurses. In those societies, the child is kept close to infancy, as in the Samoa of the 1920s, where Mead found the child was taught to respond to the rhythms and cycles of his body; or in Bali, where the child learns to act out his terror through dramatics; or in Iatmul, where he learns to retain his passivity within an energetic and often angry adult society. Perhaps the closest model of child-oriented education of this type in our society is the Montessori school, where even the furniture is adapted to fit the shape and needs of the child, and where the teacher literally gets down to the child's level.

Contrasting sharply with that model is the society in which children are reared by grandparents, as in the case of the North American Plains Indians, of whom Mead had personal experience with the Omaha. Here, the grandparent-as-teacher transmits a much different message to the child from that of the older-sister-as-teacher. The message is conservative, much as the professor in the academy extolls the virtues of stability and sobriety to be found among *his* generation to the children of men and women who share reverence for the values of the past.

Finally, there is the society in which the children are raised by their own parents, more or less the model found in contemporary middle-class American homes. From a cross-cultural perspective, Mead compared this situation to that of the Manus: the stern, goal-oriented parents forever teaching their children to be alert and ready to face a new and challenging world, much like the teacher in today's crowded city school preparing her students to set out into an uncharted world.

The problem with using these models, Mead said in "The School in American Culture," is that their application to the education problems of 1950—and presumably to those of today, as well—was limited. The problem of American education was how to teach young people to cope with rapid change. The children of 1950—and here she presages the Sputnik phenomenon—are "actually unlike any children who have ever been in the world before." Because they were growing up in an atomic age, in which technological development and scientific change would make yesterday's knowledge not merely passé, but practically useless for solving tomorrow's problems, the children of the postwar baby boom were unique. Never before had the older generation of society not possessed enough experience or knowledge to be able to counsel the younger generation; now, it was the younger generation that was growing up with a premium on experience. This, of course, is the germ of the idea of the generation gap between parents and children that Mead would develop more fully in *Culture and Commitment*. In the context of 1950, however, she limited herself to a description of the phenomenon and its effect on children and their teachers. By 1950, she said, teachers were in the unenviable position of actually knowing *less* about their students the more experience they had, so that the teacher of twenty years' experience might be less confident of her understanding of the children than a much younger teacher with only a couple of years' experience. Children's behavior was becoming less, not more, predictable, mirroring conditions in a world that was becoming increasingly disoriented and incomprehensible to the older generation. Mead said a kind of "nightmare reversal" had come about. Instead of conferring wisdom and solidity on their bearers, age and experience made people more disoriented. They simply could not understand what was going on in a world that was unlike any world ever experienced before the atomic age. The situation, she said, was like an escalator that keeps running backward.

What, then, was the prospect for the school in American culture in 1950? Despite the "nightmarish" situation, Mead was optimistic. We needed teachers, she said, who could prepare their students for the unknown, to "use *unknown* ways to solve unknown problems." This is a reiteration of an earlier essay, written during the war, in which Mead said that we "must concentrate upon teaching our children to walk so steadily that we need not hew too straight and narrow paths for them but can trust them to make new paths through difficulties we never encountered to a future of which we have no inkling today." It was to become a familiar theme of hers.

Her second major essay, "Why is Education Obsolete?," was published in the *Harvard Business Review* in the fall of 1958. What distinguishes this piece from other post-Sputnik treatises on education is that it does not prescribe a simplistic formula for achieving scientific parity with the Russians. The temptation was to play on the fears of the American public by recommending short-term solutions, such as requiring more science classes in the schools. Instead, Mead went to the crux of the problem: the outdated nature of America's schools. Building upon the argument made earlier in "The School in American Culture," Mead asserted—quite rightly, too—that the problem with American education was not *what* or *how* children were being taught but rather *why* they were being taught as they were. The American education system, she said, suffered from an incomplete understanding of its own purpose and goals. The problem, it seems, was not in our stars (or satellites) but in ourselves.

One reason why Americans were flailing about blindly trying to solve the post-Sputnik education "crisis," Mead said, was that they had fallen prey to a number of false assumptions about the schools: that the American educational system had somehow "fallen behind" its Russian counterpart, that the baby boom was causing an inordinate number of problems with the schools, and that it was time for the pendulum to swing back to more rigid, disciplined forms of teaching and classroom behavior. If these assumptions were correct, then concentrating on greater quantities or different approaches to teaching, such as requiring more science classes or hiring assistants to aid teachers, might work. Unfortunately, the assumptions were wrong because they were based on the wrong questions. Americans should have been asking such questions as: Is the system of education suited to the needs of a highly technical, rapidly changing industrial society such as America's? Could it be out of date? Do Americans understand the basic issues of education? What about the change in the *rate* of change—the fact that today, significant changes take place in years or months, not in decades or centuries as they did in the past? How can society prepare children for life in a world whose needs are totally unpredictable? Instead of finding answers to these seminal questions, Americans looked over their shoulders at the Russians.

Perhaps the reason for the nation's muddled thinking about the true nature of the problems of education, said Mead, was an incomplete understanding of today's student. In the past, the image of the student in American culture took two basic forms—the student as scholar, and the student as child-victim. As the stereotypical scholar, the student was treated as a kind of immature, perennially adolescent monk, cloistered in the study hall or classroom, unable to fend for himself in the real world, totally dependent upon society to care for his needs. The image of the student as child-victim, however, came with the Industrial Revolution, when children barely out of infancy were pressed into service in the mines and factories. The goal of child labor laws, therefore, was to get the children out of the sweatshops and into the classroom; thus was universal education born. From these two images of the student, said Mead, society created a composite picture of the function of education: to protect children from exploitation; to keep them morally and economically dependent on their elders; to provide education for all, not just the privileged; to teach complex skills, which their parents were unable to do; and to transmit the knowledge that the parents themselves might not possess (particularly in the case of immigrant families) but which they wanted their children to acquire. Thus, schools became the place where societal values were taught and where knowledge was transmitted vertically, from the elders (or their surrogates, the teachers) to the students.

That image of the school no longer remained valid, said Mead. The world was changing too rapidly. The information that the elders passed along was obsolete even before it was transmitted. The pace of change had made the problem of educating the young infinitely more complex than in the past. The vertical transmission of knowledge—from old to young—no longer was adequate. Something new had to be invented to replace it. Mead called it lateral transmission of knowledge—from those who know (no matter how young the "teacher" may be) to those who are ignorant. In a world where a nineteen-year-old may know more about the latest developments in subatomic particle theory than his elders, lateral transmission provides a continuum, or matrix, upon which knowledge can be transferred from one person to another. Old distinctions based on age no longer applied. The "teacher" is the one with knowledge, no matter what his age, and the student is the one seeking the knowledge. The only prerequisite to achieving a true education in such a context, said Mead, is the desire to know.

In this rapidly changing world, she added, the idea of "finishing" one's education was absurd. Historically, Americans have named certain guideposts as indicators of scholastic achievement that lead to success in the "real" world: a high school diploma, a college degree, the Ph.D. Today, said Mead, scholastic attainment is not sufficient in and of itself to guarantee success outside the walls of academe. The student must continually "keep up" if he hopes to keep pace with developments around him. Even nomenclature had to change. Americans must no longer think of "primary" education as that period lasting up to a certain grade level, and "secondary" education applying to the high school years. Today, primary education had to be seen as the basics of survival—knowing how to read, to do math, to understand the concepts of law, to use money. Secondary education was everything else that a person needed to know at any time in his life or in any "amount." Only by coming to grips with the nature of change could one hope to keep up with it, said Mead, for from now on, "no one will live all his life in the world into which he was born, and no one will die in the world in which he worked in his maturity."

When it came to specific reforms, some of Mead's ideas clearly were flawed by their impractical or unpolitic nature. She advocated paying students to go to college, for example, using public tax money and private donations, on the premise that going to school was a job that should be compensated. But she failed to explain fully why the advantaged few who got into college should be subsidized by the rest of society. She also felt that certain professions should be given priority or subsidies, mentioning teaching as a prime area of shortage at the time (1962), but failing to foresee that, in less than a decade, the market for teachers would be glutted. More sensible, perhaps, was her suggestion to give education vouchers to those who had successfully completed work in her proposed National Service Corps, much as the G.I. Bill provides such benefits to discharged servicemen. Of course, this proposal hinged on approval of her national service program which, whatever its merits, has never enjoyed widespread support.

Other of her ideas enjoyed greater popularity. She believed firmly that sex education should *not* be isolated from a more rounded understanding of family and human relationships and should not be a separate "course"; moreover, she said, parents should have the right to remove their children from classroom discussions of human sexuality, just as they may obtain released time for religious education. She advocated a certification process, whereby people without formal education could prove their capacity in a subject by taking examinations, a concept that is growing in acceptance today. While she believed that "coeducation is here to stay," she thought it hurt both boys and girls to be thrown together at certain delicate stages of adolescence, without accounting for differences in maturation between the sexes. The effect is to push adulthood on them before they're ready. "We put them together in high school at one period when they should have nothing to do with each other," she said. Girls soon learn to act dumb if they want to get along with boys, even though they are years ahead of them in terms of maturation; the poor boys have to worry about dating and social obligations at a time when many of them would prefer to concentrate on sports and other interests. It is for this reason that Mead advocated the abolition of the separate junior high school, where young teens were isolated in their misery, in favor of the large education complex, where youngsters in a wide range of ages and stages of physical and emotional development could find others in their own stage of development with whom to socialize. After all, said Mead, chronological age does not always correspond to emotional maturity. Many junior high school children are young and vulnerable.

The concept of building large education complexes applied to the high school, too, which Mead felt needed as much overhauling as the junior high. In her 1960 Cubberly Lecture at Stanford University, Mead questioned how well the high schools were serving America's young adults. In "The High School of the Future," she asked: Is high school a stage of education for anyone with an elementary diploma? Or is it a step that leads to a next step, perhaps to college or a job? Is it a kind of school that opens doors to new learning, or is it the end of the education line? In their desperation to understand the proper role of the high school, said Mead, Americans were forgetting that high schools, like junior high schools, are places where adolescents in various stages of growth and development are brought together. Some are young and vulnerable and need a place that is familiar and homelike, with a teacher who can help them learn the basic skills necessary to life. Others need to learn group skills and how to behave under supervision. Then there are those whose physical growth, emotional development, or social maturation is out of step with their chronological age or intellectual development. Finally, there is the mature student, whose needs are often neglected, making him feel that he is being babied or held back by high school.

All these differing needs and requirements add up to a demand for a new kind of high school, said Mead, a place that is not so much a "school" as a "setting." Such a setting might be more like a community center than a school, where high school students in various phases of growth could find access to a variety of programs and experiences and thereby feel more at home in the school environment. A high school based on the "community center" idea, she believed, would go far toward releasing some of the bitterness that young people feel toward a society that constantly demands of them, but gives little in return. Here would be a special place for them, accommodated to their needs at a time of life when awkwardness and uncertainty can make it difficult for even the most mature young people to cope.

Many of Mead's other suggestions (which are by no means exclusively hers, as she was the first to acknowledge) bear looking into. She told a congressional committee in 1970 that students should be given more opportunities for work experience programs, to combine the scholastic with the practical, particularly in public-service jobs, such as ecology; that the system of taxation to finance schools, based on the real estate tax, discriminated against children in poor districts with low real estate valuation;* that technological advances, such as teaching machines and television, deserved careful consideration by educators; that the neighborhood schools should be preserved; and that barriers between the home and the school that prevented literate parents from teaching their children should be eliminated.

Mead was also able to see that educational reform had to transcend national boundaries. Her experience as an anthropologist specializing in cultural change pushed her into the forefront of efforts to bring first-class education to the Third World. Early in her career, when she was studying the Plains Indians, an old man, one of the leaders of the Peyote cult (whose followers hallucinate on the drug to reach the spiritual world), told her of one of his visions. "My children will not need to take peyote," he told Mead, "for they will know how to read."

But teaching the world's poor to read was no mean task, as Mead knew. Just after World War II, she formulated a literacy program for the United Nations Educational, Scientific and Cultural Organization (UNESCO) in which she suggested that the emerging countries follow a three-step approach to reading, first achieving literacy in the native

---

*A few months later, the California Supreme Court ruled (in the famous *Serrano* case) that such discrimination was unconstitutional under California law, setting off a string of similar legal challenges throughout the Union.

tongue, then literacy in a language with a full literature, and, finally, introducing reading and writing into the society at the community level. The key to any such program, however, lay in coordinating the plan for education with the culture of the people being educated. That is why Mead believed it necessary to make a detailed study of the culture before applying any educational system to it, so that the literacy plan could be made part of the culture's system of incentives and sanctions. Moreover, any international literacy plan of the type Mead envisioned in 1947 had to have several prerequisites. First, the "higher" culture being brought to the less-developed area must be made as widely available as possible, within as short a time period as possible. It must also make the people who are to benefit from it functional within today's technological world. Finally, it must place a high value on achieving health and longevity for the people in question. Otherwise, Mead said, the plan would fail.

Unfortunately, the high ideals of Mead's proposal were somewhat distorted in practice, largely because of a misconception of what worldwide education is all about. As Mead explained, "adult education" for the world's masses at first was thought of as a kind of catch-up program for the "underprivileged" who had been denied access to their "rightful" share of education. The solution: a kind of "classics in translation" approach, passing on a watered-down version of Western culture. Then, adult education came to mean a "fundamental" education, one in which the "established" order tried to "modernize" the peasant class in the hope that, having read Shakespeare, the natives might be induced to wear "civilized" clothing or relinquish some savage practice. Teaching the poor "fundamentals" might also make them more accepting of modern sanitation, medicine, and technology, and thus a little more controllable in the hands of the European authorities. Ultimately, adult education took on the meaning of a sort of "gap" between the rich nations and the poor, a gap, incidentally, that some thought could never be closed. How would it be possible, the postwar pessimists said, for the underdeveloped nations to approach the level of education achieved in the industrialized countries?

Yet, upon her return to Manus in 1953, Mead herself realized how wrong it was to believe that the people of the Third World necessarily had to be limited in their potential achievement. At the same time, she modified her conclusions from her original voyage in 1928. When she first studied the Manus children, with their free and open attitude toward life, she wondered how they could turn into the hard, toughened Manus adult. From this observation, she concluded that lasting change cannot be achieved primarily by education, but must first come through a change in society. By 1953, she was prepared to see, from the tremendous cultural change the Manus had undergone during the war (notably from the flood of American GIs) that it is possible to "implant" certain yearnings in youths which, under specific conditions, manifest themselves as cultural attributes when they become adults. In simple terms, Mead learned that in today's rapidly evolving world, change need not take two generations or more to be made part of a culture. The Manus had completely modernized in just twenty-five years.

In fact, the question of world education could not, in Mead's estimation, be condensed into a simple characterization of a struggle between the rich countries and the poor. Today, no society can be content to remain static when it comes to education. We are all students. The rich no less than the poor must come to see that education is really a reaction to change, change that is occurring so fast that it requires a supreme effort—whether for the scholar at an American university or for the agricultural supervisor on a plantation in the Caribbean—just to keep up with it. Gone are the days when a person could be called educated for merely mastering a certain body of knowledge. Nowadays, the truly educated person is one who admits his ignorance and is willing to adapt to what Mead called the "experience and expectation of change." Children must be taught to learn not by rote, but by understanding the very *nature* of the subjects at hand: to learn, not Latin or Spanish, for example, but the nature of language, so that they can be prepared to learn *any* language—for who knows what language they will "need" when they are adults?

As for adults, they, too, will have to engage in a new and endless form of continuing education, one that puts a premium on the adult who, as Mead put it, can make a "swift transference" from an old idea to a new generalization. Those who hold firm to the belief that they have "acquired" enough knowledge to anticipate any situation will soon find themselves swept away by the winds of change. For both children and adults, therefore, the future belongs to those who understand that it is not *what* one learns, but *how* one learns, that counts, whether one lives in a primitive or postindustrial society. The education gap, said Mead, is not strictly between the rich countries and the poor countries; it is between today and tomorrow.

6
Feminism and Beyond

Fame alone cannot account for Margaret Mead's popularity with women. She was a living example of women's liberation—a "brilliant exception," she would mockingly say of herself—long before that phrase came into vogue. She climbed to the top in a field that once had been almost exclusively a male bastion. Women of all ages and backgrounds could look up to her as a model of professionalism—the consummate career woman. But her role was not limited to that of the solitary crusader, tilting at the windmills of male dominion. Women could identify with her as a wife and mother, if a somewhat unconventional one, given her three divorces. The average woman could sense that Mead had a personal stake in their more mundane problems: Even with all her degrees and honors, they felt, she knew how to change a diaper. In later years, the bond between Mead and her women followers grew even closer as she became a kind of benevolent grandmother figure, an interpreter and analyst of matters of concern to women—birth control, the population explosion, the generation gap, their position in the home and in society. Through her monthly column in *Redbook,* her books, and her lectures, Mead was able to provide a warm and comforting shoulder for the women of America to lean on.

Mead was no latecomer to the struggle for women's rights. As early as 1946, she was writing that the situation with regard to women was "explosive and potentially harmful." Citing a survey by *Fortune* magazine, she noted that a quarter of the women in the United States were "disturbed" about their position in society and unhappy with the isolated life of the homemaker. Both sexes were concerned about whether women should work, she noted, and were "confused, uncertain, and discontented with the present definition of women's place in America." She pointed out the "enormous contradiction" our society imposes on young girls: In school, they are taught to aspire to the same values as boys—"variety, choice, freedom"—but when they become adults, the only option is marriage and motherhood. In this and other essays written shortly after the war, Mead called for a new climate of opinion, in which women would be treated as individual persons, not solely as wives and mothers, and in which men would participate more fully in the life of the home—not simply washing the dishes, but taking on greater responsibility for the caring and nurturing necessary to keep a home happy, tasks which traditionally fell on the women. "This world must be reshaped, by both sexes, to suit the needs of both sexes," she wrote.

It is not surprising that Mead should have embraced such views, given her background. She had been raised in a home where it was assumed that a woman could be a wife and mother and still have interests outside the home. Yet even in those early writings, Mead challenged women to go beyond a mere redress of grievances—the right to work, equal pay, and similar demands that would become the familiar litany of a later generation of feminists. It was not enough to copy what men had done with the world, she said. Women must find "new patterns" to the world of work and outside society, using the unique gifts and qualities that they brought to their traditional role in the home. Those early essays are a portent of her later criticism of certain aspects of the women's liberation movement of the 1960s and 1970s.

To begin to grasp Mead's views on the position of women in society, it is necessary, as she was wont to do, to trace the evolution of woman's role. Actually, Mead preferred to avoid the phrase "the position of women in society," since it implied that women exist in a vacuum. "All of society is keyed to a relationship between the sexes and any change in the so-called position of one affects the other," she said. It makes far more sense to talk about the relationship between the sexes than about the position of one or the other, since one affects the other.

From the beginning of time, woman's place was defined in her relationship to man's place. Since only women could bear children, it was necessary, given the rate of infant death, for women to bear as many children as possible. Moreover, due to their smaller physical stature and their virtually uninterrupted condition of pregnancy, women were less suited to hunting, warfare, and other physical activities than men. Thus developed the traditional division of responsibility between the sexes, with men performing those tasks outside the home and women devoting themselves to activities within the home.

Within this construct what men did came to be valued more highly than what women did. "Every single culture that has ever existed has valued the male activities more than the female," Mead noted. "It did not make any difference what these activities were—even dressing dolls—if the men did them, they were valuable." In certain cases, as in Tchambuli society, women appeared to have less power, although in fact they wielded quite a lot; yet in a ritualistic way, they had to defer to the men. Still, the number of primitive or developed societies in which women exercised more power than men is few.

The first significant shift in this relationship came with the advent of agriculture, particularly the invention of the plow. This relieved the elite or royal members of the society from the burden of hunting and gathering food, freeing them to engage in such activities as the arts and thereby laying the basis for civilization and culture. The agricultural revolution had little effect on women, though, since even queens were valued solely for their ability to produce heirs, not for their potential contribution to the larger world.

This relative positioning of the sexes remained static until fairly recent times and remains so today over vast portions of the globe. In the more advanced societies of the western world, however, the Industrial Revolution signaled another change in the relationship between men and women. Under the emerging theory of Marx and other social reformers, women were linked with peasants and workers and treated as an oppressed class. Women made some gains for individuality and the right to a life outside the home, but mostly in cases where they were destitute and had to work. They were paid poorly and treated savagely, "legally disadvantaged and punished in a hundred ways when they insisted on being regarded as people, individuals instead of just women," said Mead. In the long run, women as a group made little progress during this period. "Although civilization had immensely enriched the lives of women, the range of women's contributions has changed remarkably little from the time when human beings first reared their children in family groups." Women were still treated as chattel, and wives were considered their husbands' property. Married women were not allowed to own property, and even the children were considered the man's possessions, not the wife's. If the Industrial Revolution freed still more men from the necessity of daily production, giving them time and opportunity to shape the larger world, it had no such liberating effect on women.

Even so, rumblings of discontent could be heard. In the United States, the first modern conference on women's rights, the Seneca Falls Convention, held in 1848, heralded the beginning of the suffragist movement in America, culminating in the passage of the Women's Suffrage Amendment and the creation of the Women's Bureau of the U.S. Department of Labor in 1920. Yet until World War I, when the contribution of women to the work force was formally recognized (with the establishment of the Women-in-Industry Service in 1918), there were really only two ways of life for women in the United States. One was a kind of formalized spinsterhood. There were several options—a religious life, companionship with another woman, such as a sister or an aunt, or boarding with a family of relatives. An unmarried woman became part of a larger community (such as a religious order) or joined a family, serving as the helpful maiden aunt who was always there in an emergency, or simply providing an extra pair of hands around the house. Spinsters were also able to pursue limited activities outside the home. "A great proportion of the women who pioneered in women's education and in new occupations were spinsters by temperament and choice," Mead noted. "In their day, chastity and virginity were respected; a woman who chose to remain single was not branded as peculiar." A life devoid of male companionship was a respected choice. And spinsters in America were not considered "masculine," as they were in Britain.

The only other choice was marriage and motherhood. In the United States, the role of the wife and mother developed in a curious and unique way. American women have always been more independent than women in any other country or culture. In some respects this was due to the process of selection, for a good portion of the women who emigrated to America did so at considerable risk. "A certain kind of girl was willing to come to America, another kind wanted to stay home with mother," said Mead. The common characteristic of these women was bravery: "they weren't frightened; they weren't afraid of facing new conditions; they weren't afraid of hardship; they weren't afraid that they might be left alone." This process of selection, coupled with the reality that a woman might indeed be left alone by her husband's death at the hands of Indians or through some other catastrophe, sparked a fierce sense of independence among American women. They became, in Mead's terms, "managers," someone with a job to do— within the house—and who did it. What developed was a "reasonable partnership" between men and women: "She had her domain, he had his. He went out, she stayed in. She told him what he could do in the house, and he told her what she couldn't do outside the house." In an emergency, the woman was prepared to take over her husband's job. For the most part, she ran her own domain with a gloved but hardly delicate hand. This was no "soft, pliant, responsive creature who was interested in listening and catering to other people's moods," wrote Mead. "She managed the house and fed her husband and her children and the [workers] the way she might have managed a large cafeteria." Despite the independence she enjoyed within her own orbit, the American woman was still tied to the home. The idea of securing rights for herself was inconceivable to her.

The first cries for reasonable treatment of women, according to Mead, were made by two groups of women who fell outside the normal range of life-styles. One was that group of homeless spinsters who had to fend for themselves. Without a system of support, these women were forced to work under discriminatory conditions. Thus, securing certain rights and protections for this group became part of the emerging women's rights platform of the late 19th and early 20th centuries. The other group was the activists, "women who wanted to get out there and fix things, who were concerned about peace, prohibition, antislavery, who wanted to take their ideas from the home out into the community." Although hampered by their condition as wives and mothers, they still pressed for social reform for women, in chief the right to vote.

But the much-sought-for franchise did not prove to be the panacea the suffragists thought it would be. Again, conditions in society had a profound effect on the position and status of women. Despite their having won the right to vote, many ambitious young women, eager for reform, met with a hostile reception in both the work world and society, where marriage and family were considered the norm for young women. "Many of those whose ambitions had been stirred found their commitment to some specialty lessened their chances for any association with men," Mead noted. They lost out on courtship and marriage and became social outcasts. Not even during the Depression, when many couples had to postpone marriage or having children, did this emphasis on marriage and the home lose its appeal. If anything, abstinence reinforced the supremacy of marriage and the home for both women and men to the extent that, during and after World War II, couples rushed into marriage with the hope of having children soon, and in quantity.

Thus, from the granting of suffrage until after the war, the agenda for women's rights was sacrificed to a series of compromises accountable to conditions in the larger society. By the 1950s, as women entered the fourth decade of supposed political equality with men, their situation had not advanced much beyond what it had been a hundred years before and in some respects was worse. In the late 19th century, a wife and mother not only was treated with respect and dignity, but had a clearly defined position in society; moreover, she often had the help of servants or other women—her mother, an aunt, a spinster, a daughter—to share the household chores and the upbringing of the younger children. The typical American woman of the 1950s, by contrast, lived in a kind of physical and psychological limbo. Instead of pursuing the opportunity for individual development toward which the general trend of women's rights seemed pointed, most women "seemed to be retreating from active participation in the wider society." Instead of postponing marriage to develop their own careers, they practically leaped into early marriage; instead of pursuing higher education, they devoted themselves to supporting and nurturing their husbands. In fact, the number of women in graduate school actually dropped during that period.

The typical housewife was isolated in her own single-family home on a half acre of suburbia, removed from any companionship or intellectually stimulating activity. Her servants were no longer the maid and cook of her grandmother's day, but the washer-dryer combination of the appliance era. "Hoover" was no longer the name of the butler, but the name of the vacuum cleaner. Even some of the activities that previously offered intense pleasure to women, such as breast feeding, were no longer necessary, thanks to formulas and bottles; and the preparation of baby food and meals for the rest of the family was made superfluous by the manufacture of fast foods. Woman became the ultimate consumer.

The upshot was that the typical suburban American housewife of midcentury was restless and unhappy. She had everything—a home, two cars, a husband, a family, gadgets galore, the highest standard of living in history. She was the envy of women around the world. But in reality, Mead found, the American woman of this period was a prisoner in her own home. "Today, the wealthiest nation in the world regards as normal and desirable a style of life for women that is only technically superior to that of medieval woman," she said in 1965. American women were overworked, trying to be not only wife and mother, but also chauffeur, maid, laundress, and hostess. Of course, by that time, women had political and economic rights. They could vote, run for office, get a job. But in the 1950s and early 1960s, these were hardly realistic options. A woman was expected to be married, to be part of a couple first and a mother second. She was not expected to be a person in her own right but had to "learn to prune and pare her personality, to make herself the less demanding, less individual member of a couple." She had, in other words, all the basic rights, "except the right to dedicate [herself] to any task other than homemaking." Even some of the old possibilities, such as spinsterhood, a religious life, or living with parents or another woman, were looked upon with disfavor. The only true fulfillment for a woman was in marriage and family, which of course depended on a relationship with a man. "Nothing that she does herself will help to make her happy," noted Mead.

Worst of all, the American woman had to measure up to an impossible standard. Every day, she saw herself compared to the ideal woman portrayed in advertisements and the movies, on television and radio—young, attractive, vibrant, yet still a perfect mother and homemaker, a model of efficiency and demeanor. If economic necessity forced her to work—the case with more and more women, as the cost of maintaining a way of life dependent on expensive gadgets rose steadily—she was nonetheless expected to continue to carry out her other, more "important" duties, with or without any extra help. Life for her was a constant struggle to keep up with these excessive demands, whether or not she liked it.

Few women could measure up to such standards. For women who

were unmarried, divorced, beyond their childbearing years, or unable to conceive, the task was impossible. If the woman had a job, rarely was it fulfilling in itself. It was just that, a job, not a career or profession, and it had to be done in addition to her household tasks, which had priority. Not only was she constantly measured against the image of perfection portrayed in the media, but her achievement depended on how well she made her husband and children happy. Moreover, the prospects for achieving happiness declined as her physical beauty and her ability to have children diminished. Mead described this sad state of affairs eloquently as "years and years of lesserness." And yet, there was little the average woman could do. Her self-esteem depended on how much she made others happy, not herself. The result was a kind of perverted set of demands. "In her search for success she demands more *of* herself if she is self-conscious and aware; *for* herself if she is less sophisticated," said Mead.

The dilemma for women, then, was that society's view of their role was determined largely by men's view of the world, in which women "adapt, cope, and make do." Not that this situation was necessarily good for men, since it separated them from their families and possibly damaged their health. But this was the context in which the women's movement of the late 1960s was formed, and in which Mead figured as advocate, interpreter, and *grande dame*. It explains to a great extent why women in the latter third of the 20th century would make the kinds of demands they did, and it supplies some insight into why some of the more strident themes in the feminist repertory hit a discordant note with a large sector of American womanhood.

The women's liberation movement, according to Mead, was built on several major grievances—the obvious inequality of opportunity between women and men, the lack of free choice for women, and discrimination in jobs and education. These became apparent in the 1960s, when women were more or less thrust into the work force to fill the need for cheap, educated labor. Women, particularly those of middle age whose children were out of the home, were told that their lives were "unfulfilled," when actually they were needed to fill dead-end positions as secretaries, typists, and other low-level clerical jobs. Many others had to take jobs because the escalating standard of living made it impossible for men to support their families on one income alone. As for women with children, they were "apparently supposed to raise their babies in the middle of the night."

Besides the actual legal and economic restrictions against women,

Mead found insidious a "style of life that made it more difficult for women [than for men] to attain any degree of success in the business world." Women were expected to subjugate their jobs to their roles as wives and mothers. Going to the very essence of women's role in society, each woman in the 1960s was forced "to decide who and what she is against a montage of millions of other people's images, disseminated in a world still majorly controlled by men." All women, whether or not they worked at an outside job, were burdened by a whole array of managerial and maintenance chores in the home, which severely limited their ability to do the things that *they* might want to do. The feminist movement, therefore, was "primarily a movement of women who were reduced to being nothing but consumers, making consumer choices and having no chance to be productive at all."

Still another factor in the women's rights movement was the Freudian interpretation of male and female roles. As Mead saw it, Freud was so bound up in his own 19th-century European interpretation of culture that he failed to consider how sexuality could be viewed under different conditions. Freud believed that biological makeup determined one's role in society, that "anatomy is destiny." In his view females suffered from penis envy, and Freud interpreted as a drive to be masculine any attempt by women to defy the "anatomy is destiny" principle or to transcend the traditional role of wife and mother by demanding to be treated as a person. Carried to its logical conclusion, Freud's interpretation meant that any organized effort by women to attain equality was simply further evidence of their attempt to overcome penis envy.

Mead's argument against Freud is based on her understanding of non-European cultures, both primitive and modern. What Freud ignored, said Mead, was that "the social definition of male and female roles throughout prehistory and history have reflected practical conditions." The necessity for women to breast feed and carry infants and for men to spend virtually all their time providing for their families accounted for the traditional division of responsibility, not penis envy. When conditions in society changed, as they did with the invention of agriculture and the coming of the Industrial Revolution, the relationship between male and female roles changed, too, although less favorably for women than for men. Moreover, said Mead, Freud failed to grasp that boys and girls in other cultures, such as those

Mead had studied in Oceania (and which formed the basis for her argument in *Male and Female*), could see "anatomy is destiny" in a different way. In open societies such as these, said Mead, the evidence of sexual difference is apparent to children of both sexes from an early age. Boys see girls menstruate, develop breasts, carry children; girls see boys' penises and see them have erections. From an early age, girls accept their femininity and their potentiality for having children; boys understand their inability to bear children, and put their emphasis on achievement. If Freud could postulate penis envy, said Mead, there is ample evidence from other cultures to indicate womb envy among males. Thus, "there is no more reason for a girl to envy a boy than for a boy to envy a girl, for the contrasting and differentiated functions of each are fully apparent to children of each sex."

Mead was sufficiently generous in her critique to point out that Freud was writing when there was little work done on children and on the kinds of cross-cultural analyses that later researchers, including Mead herself, could bring to the discussion. But she could not dismiss the effect of Freud's interpretation of female sexuality on modern-day attitudes, particularly as they affected the attainment of equal rights for women. For Freud's theory of female penis envy, with its corollary that for women to assert themselves as individuals was merely an expression of a perverse desire to be "masculine," had infected current thinking about the women's movement. "Thus," she wrote in 1974, "the century and a half of feminism through which we have just gone has witnessed a continuing interpretation of psycho-sexual development as females suffering from the discovery that they were not born males and free."

But for all her sympathy with the cause of women's liberation, Mead thought it too anti-male. "The emphasis is stridently on women's rights for women's sake," she said, labeling the more radical members of the movement "conspicuously self-centered and hostile to men." The result was that more heat than light was being produced. "The whole process of change is taking place in an atmosphere of the greatest bad temper and a tremendous amount of secondary hostility is being generated that in itself poses a threat to a good outcome," she said. To blame men entirely for the problems of women was, she thought, "a vast oversimplification," for women "cannot build on the fantasy that [they] have been held down by a conspiracy." The women's movement described women as "handicapped" by history and biology and placed its primary emphasis on removing these disabilities. "Wherever women in any way differ from men, . . . there is a demand that society should make up for the difference," she wrote. "The view of equality is, therefore, that anything in woman's biological nature which prevents her from having full expression outside the home . . . should be compensated for." Thus, if women have to bear children, society should arrange for the children's care so that women will be free to pursue their own interests. Yet the feminist solution is merely to "turn a contemporary picture of the masculine world into a feminine daydream of the future," to reshape the world using "masculine qualities interpreted in a kind of caricature by women." Mead also felt that too many women were undergoing "consciousness raising" without understanding how to manage it properly. She was disturbed, too, by the lesbian overtones of the radical fringe. Lesbianism was fine, she said, as long as it was a personal choice; but when it was based purely on sexual politics, it was insulting.

The radical feminist agenda was, therefore, both inadequate and shortsighted, from Mead's point of view. It placed the blame for women's position squarely on the shoulders of men, without considering why "most women still cling tenaciously to age-old feminine aspirations" of marriage and family. More to the point, the feminist platform simply offered no potential for truly revolutionary change. It sought to compensate for women's supposed handicaps, without offering a vision of male-female relationships for tomorrow's world. A simple reversal of sex roles, Mead felt certain, would "bring us no closer to the development of styles of relationships that will foster the full humanity of both men and women." This eradication of sexual differences was "an old nightmare turned into a silly feminist dream, and a bad one." As for the Equal Rights Amendment, Mead said the concept was "fine when applied to race, but if it reaches the point at which it leads us to ignore the fact that men and women *are different,* we'll further injure both sexes."

What the radical feminists failed to grasp was how to apply the special characteristics and capacities of women to the needs of today's changing world: "Can we use our knowledge to think ahead, as the most imaginative men in earlier civilizations could not do, and visualize how women can use their gifts, so long centered on the home, to create a more human world?" she asked. The women's liberation movement also failed to look to a future world in which childbearing, child rearing, and homemaking are no longer the central focus of women's lives.

Mead's disaffection with this unsophisticated approach to women's liberation is most apparent in her criticism of the Report of the President's Commission on the Status of Women. In 1963, President Kennedy's blue-ribbon panel issued a report supporting virtually all the demands of the nascent women's movement—equal opportunity for women in job hiring, training, and promotion; equal educational opportunity; child-care programs; equal treatment under the law; a basic homemaker's income under the Social Security system; and numerous other reforms, many of which have since been enacted into law, if not fully realized in fact. Mead had no quarrel with the majority of these recommendations, having supported them for years. Her dispute was more with the character and extent of the recommendations. The commission, she wrote, had stopped short of writing a complete report on the status of women.

The major technical shortcoming of the report, Mead said, was that it ignored the role of the woman in the home. There was "no real recognition of the principal historical difference between women's and men's roles"—that "while men generally have devoted themselves to organizing and exploiting the outside world of nature and society, women have devoted most of their time and attention to the care and well-being of individuals, primarily to their families." In Mead's view, the report overemphasized the potential of women in the work force to the detriment of their role in the home. The report assumed that most women wanted to work, yet the commission could not deny that, while many women are forced to take jobs, "the women who have a choice . . . are choosing for the home." Not enough was said about those women.

In fact, for a report that was supposed to help reduce prejudice about women, it contained a number of untested assumptions that ultimately tainted its recommendations, Mead noted. First, it assumed that "anything peculiarly feminine is a handicap," especially in comparison to the ideal of the educated, white Anglo-Saxon male. It further assumed that "both men and women attain full biological humanity only through marriage and children," yet sex, marriage, and parenthood should have no sacrifices attached to them. Finally, the report stressed that "the right to work at a paid job is an intrinsic condition of human dignity" and implied, therefore, that homemaking is not an acceptable alternative. In short, the commission's report assumed that most women, given the choice, would prefer to work outside the home and that any obstacles to this choice—such as the birth of a child, the need to care for a member of the family, or even an individual woman's personal choice—must be eliminated.

But, said Mead, just as Freud put too much emphasis on penis envy to explain women's status in society, the President's Commission put too small a value on matters of intrinsic significance to women. Why else would women, having achieved the right to vote and work and having proven their ability to perform all sorts of jobs during World War II, opt for a life devoted to homemaking in the 1950s? This phenomenon, said Mead, "suggests that other very important factors affect the position of women and the choices they make, factors that will not be altered by the removal of legal, educational, and economic handicaps alone." Conditions in society have too strong an influence on male-female relationships to be ignored. The same generation of women who glorified the nuclear family and the half-acre world of the suburbs were a decade later railing against the limitations and hardships of homemaking and demanding the right to work outside the home, a choice they viewed as more glamorous and stimulating than homemaking. But, asked Mead, "is this an expression of anything more than another swing of the pendulum?" Would the women of the 1960s, focused as they were on the achievement in the outside world, learn to their own and society's regret that other parts of their lives had been neglected? Or that some women were being pushed into dead-end jobs—not careers—because of a societal pressure that equated outside employment with fulfillment? To force women to work who might otherwise choose a life devoted to the home or in some other "caring" occupation (such as a solitary religious life) would, in Mead's view, be as wrong as denying women the right to work, if that is their *real* choice, not one dictated by society. "The pendulum must not swing too far, forcing out of the home women whose major creative life is grounded in motherhood and wifehood," she said.

In sum, the President's Commission on the Status of Women had gone too far in one direction, to the detriment of other matters vital to women. "By concentrating primarily on women as workers . . . the report has obscured issues central to its subject," Mead said. If the kinds of "caring" activities that have always been the domain of women are stripped of dignity and meaning, who in society will perform these tasks? "Who . . . will be free to care—with continuity—for human beings?" asked Mead. "Who will devote themselves to the persistent daily needs for companionship, sympathy and warmth?" If homemaking and other human-care activities are looked upon as denying women dignity and choice because they don't have a salary attached to them, said Mead, then society had better prepare someone else to take over these activities, or suffer the consequences, for "the present homemaking style can be attained and maintained only when another woman, or a man, replaces the homemaker. . . ." By ignoring the homemaking and caring functions of women, and particularly by failing to suggest feasible and dignified options to women who choose a life concentrated on the home, the President's Commission, in Mead's view, had raised hopes for the "liberation" of some, but by no means all, women.

The women's movement as described in the commission report could hardly be viewed as revolutionary, said Mead, noting that we are in the midst of a revolution of immense proportions—a revolution in birth control, which allows women to control the number and spacing of children, and in medical technology, which has drastically reduced the rate of infant mortality in industrialized countries. The result, Mead said, is that "this is the first time in history that society has not been scared to death that there would not be enough children." At the same time, we face the real and present danger of overpopulation in the nonindustrialized world, with the specter of famine, energy and resource shortages, and killing pollution, not to mention war.

It is in this larger context that women's liberation must be placed, according to Mead. With the medical revolution occurring side by side with the population explosion, the traditional division of responsibilities based on sex is no longer valid—or even desirable. Women must assume a larger role than merely using their unique gifts of nurturing and caring (that is, conservation) to change the world for the better—and not just into a feminist version of the present situation. "Can't we add something," asked Mead, "and not merely demand half of what is?"

These revolutionary changes thrust women into a tremendous position of responsibility. "The world is in a position in which it needs what women can contribute," said Mead. It is necessary for women "to right things that are so terribly wrong in the world" (such as pollution, the spread of toxic substances, the threat of a nuclear disaster) and to care "earnestly and vigorously for the future of our children, our loved country, the culture and language and religious facts we care about."

The crisis, then, as Mead saw it, was one of the imagination—how society, and particularly women, could use their talents and gifts to deal with the problems of population growth, changing interpersonal relations, and diminishing resources. "The crucial question today, I believe, is how we shall begin to reorder our lives so that having a smaller number of children can enrich the lives of both children and adults," she said in 1970. The answer, she said, was to apply the special gifts of nurturing and conservation that women have always brought to their tasks: "We can only save our own children by saving other people's children." It is up to women to examine how men had gone wrong in organizing the world and to bring their unique talents to bear on these problems. "Then the feminine preference for persons, for caretaking and conservation, for intimacy of understanding *combined with* the masculine preference for working with things, for mastery and exploitation, for rational objectivity, can enrich our perceptions of the world." Most important, it is crucial for women to realize that they must not be content merely to inherit the world from men. They must change it for the better.

Such a turnabout cannot be expected to take place immediately, or even in the space of one generation. But already there are positive signs that women are ready to face their responsibility for building a new world, as evidenced by the growing number of choices available to them. For example, many young couples are considering a variety of new marital alternatives: marriage, with only one child; marriage, with adoption of children; marriage with no children, where either both partners concentrate on full-time careers, or the woman devotes herself, as in more traditional times, to the interests of her husband. This new outlook also presents a broader set of options for women who, in earlier times, might have been excluded from active participation in society—women beyond the child-bearing years and women who chose not to marry, particularly (for the latter) those women who have, in Mead's words, chosen a life of "single blessedness" in religion, the arts, science, or statesmanship. A changed perspective on women's roles also opens the door for young mothers to see a future beyond their childbearing years, a future bright with opportunity for them to apply the skills and talents of caring and nurturing to the affairs of the world. And for those who choose the traditional path of marriage and motherhood, there will be wider options and choices, both during and after the childbearing years.

Thus, said Mead, in this brave new world, the traditional feminine styles of life based on the nuclear family may be somewhat attenuated in the greater interest of keeping the population explosion under control. While some women may feel deprived of direct experience with childbirth and the raising of children, their opportunities for participation in the outside world grow every day. "The most intense wishes of women for self-fulfillment will not outweigh their need for warmth and intimacy," said Mead. "But we can, if we will, build on this need in other ways than through the old association with bringing up children." Women can, in effect, adopt the children of the world—both this and the next generation—as their own. To build this new image of womanhood, however, a young woman must be taught that marriage is *not* the only possible state for women and men, but that "other devotions," as she called them—to work, art, science, society, or God—are possible. "We must teach them the richness of the world around them," she said, "and in doing this, we need to remember that there are other ways of having children beyond bearing them and caring for them."

This new and greater role for women, which goes well beyond that suggested by the feminists, can be the start of a new era of broadened freedoms for both sexes. As early as 1944, Mead noted that "every step that women make towards real freedom—which includes freedom to play as feminine a role as they are able to play—frees men too." Both men and women, she said, "need liberation from a life-style that is stultifying and destructive to both sexes." Instead of the climate of anger surrounding the demands of the women's movement, Mead foresaw a new atmosphere, based on already-emerging complementary roles, which not only will give women greater individual choice and a more gratifying sense of themselves, but will benefit men, too. A society that denies choice to women also strips men of their options, because "the good life for one sex is dependent upon the good life for the other, also. In those cultures where the lives of women are more narrowly restricted, the lives of the men are correspondingly restricted."

"Every time we liberate a woman, we liberate a man," she wrote.

As civilization has developed, she noted, more and more people have been freed to devote themselves to improve society. "Now, as never before, we need the imagination, the dedication, the creativity of everyone, to get society through the massive transformation in values and institutions required for an interdependent, diversified, mutually respecting and supportive planetary society." Humankind, she concluded, "has never had such a challenge before."

And it is not merely women who gain from true women's liberation. Society gains, too. Where in past generations "half of the best minds were consumed in the performance of small domestic tasks, society can now draw on them." Thus, more is at stake in the ultimate liberation of women than merely achieving equal opportunity between the sexes. The future of our society may depend on whether women, with their special gifts and talents, are integrated into a world previously reserved for men.

Judged from the perspective of her whole body of thought on the status of women, Mead emerges as more than a mere feminist. Her eye was not merely on obtaining rights for her sex, but for their exercising responsibility, too. Of herself, she said, "In a sense, I was never a feminist. I made friends of women. I stood by women, and if I was asked to do something that might improve the position of women in general, I did it. But I've never had a chip on my shoulder." That is why it can be said that Mead was a humanist first and a feminist when necessary. She put the needs of the world before any narrow concerns of her sex.

7
This Island Earth

At a high-level conference she once attended, Margaret Mead heard a representative of an international aid group tell how his agency was going to pour millions of dollars of assistance into a certain undeveloped region of the world. "You know, it's clear sailing," he told the conferees. "We understand the resources, the technology, and what we need to do. The only thing that seems to be difficult is the people."

In the period after World War II, solutions to such complex problems as feeding the world's poor, improving the economies of undeveloped countries, and generally raising the living standards of all peoples indeed seemed near at hand, in the opinion of many experts. India would be modernized in fifteen years, China in ten. With the vast technological resources at its command, not the least of them the awesome power of the atom, the Western world was confident it could link its expertise and capital with the natural resources of the undeveloped countries to bring the Third World into the modern age.

After more than three decades of effort, however, the bold predictions of the postwar period have fallen far short. If anything, conditions are worse today than in the bleakest days just after the war. In 1975, Mead described the situation thus: "We know that it has not turned out the way we expected; more people are suffering and enormously more are unhappy and feel aggrieved and oppressed than ever before."

What had gone wrong? At least three things. The first had to do with what Mead called the "human component." Like the specialist who had everything programmed except the people, the experts in economic development and international aid had forgotten to plug the human component into their computer models. By failing to take stock of the culture and background of the people in need—the very considerations that an anthropologist would make primary—the "experts" doomed their plans to certain rejection by those people they were supposed to be helping.

The second point had to do with the threat to the earth's natural resources and ecological systems—to the air, the water, the land, and life itself. It is worth noting that as late as 1962, when Rachel Carson published *Silent Spring,* her chilling exposé on DDT, "ecology" was an unfamiliar term to all but a small group of naturalists and scientists. By the end of the 1960s, the environmental crisis—with its consequences for energy usage and international development—would be a household term.

The third point had to do with technology itself—or, more accurately, our understanding of its limits. In the postwar period, most experts assumed that high-level technology would have the same unbounded benefits for the people of Quito and Peking as it had had for the inhabitants of New York and Moscow. The only problem the experts could see was getting the technology *to* the undeveloped countries. Not enough of the experts understood that new technology often is accompanied by an unforeseen threat to the environment or a radical change in the culture of a people—side effects that sometimes cause more problems than they solve.

By the 1970s, these shortcomings had combined to dash the West's great expectations for world progress. As Mead commented in 1975, the "extravagant hopes" that high technology, mechanized agriculture, and Western forms of political organization could somehow be "grafted" onto the traditional behavior of the world's rural and tribal peoples, and "the belief that somehow the rest of the world should stand still, while the economically disadvantaged caught up—it has all turned out so differently." The energy and environmental crisis made it clear to Mead that "the whole system [had] blown up so fast that nobody fully realized what was happening, nobody took responsibility, and we didn't have any way of looking at [the problem] as a whole."

Yet even into the 1960s, when photographs beamed back from space made concrete the unity of mankind, the so-called experts continued to put their faith in small-scale, one-shot solutions to complex, intertwined problems. The popular metaphor of the day compared the earth to a giant spaceship—an inept comparison, according to Mead. The earth is more like a small, delicate island adrift in the universe. "We are all living on a planet that we can now know as men once knew small islands," she wrote. Like modern-day Robinson Crusoes, the inhabitants of island Earth must conserve resources; but unlike Crusoe, who had only Friday to worry about, today's island dwellers must also find shared values to solve common problems. "Only if we see we are all in it, every one of us . . . , can something be done," said Mead.

It took the Arab oil embargo of 1974 to alert the United States in particular to the worldwide nature of the energy/environment crisis. "Suddenly the message has come across loud and clear: We are living beyond our means," Mead wrote at the time. "Americans," she said, "have developed a life-style that is draining the earth of its priceless and irreplaceable resources without regard for the future of our children and the people all around the world." The energy crisis unleashed a whole panoply of threats—worldwide famine, environmental catastrophe, even global war. Clearly there was need for leadership to sort out the situation.

From her experience in dealing with nutrition, changing cultural patterns, and international organizations, Mead became one of the strong voices in a chorus of scientists and experts devoted to seeking long-term solutions—people like Barry Commoner, René Dubos, Constantinos Doxiadis, and Barbara Ward. For years, she had devoted herself increasingly to these matters, serving as a member of the World Council of Churches committee on man's future, cochairman of the U.S. Task Force on the Future of Mankind, president of both the Scientists Institute for Public Information and the World Society for Ekistics, and representative to various United Nations conferences, including the 1972 U.N. Conference on the Human Environment in Stockholm.

In talking about the environment, Mead stressed the shared nature of the problem and the necessity for joint action to solve it. Nowhere was the need for a unified front more apparent than in the threat to what Mead called "the shared atmosphere." "Our shared atmosphere," she wrote, "so fragile, so subject to pollution and contamination, this air we breathe together, gives us a new realm in which to develop far beyond our development so far." Today, the knowledge of the shared atmosphere makes man "begin to think of all human beings on this planet as those whose fate and future are inextricably bound up with [his] own."

But no specific threat to the environment—not even a nuclear disaster, or the development of the liquid-metal fast-breeder reactor, which Mead called "probably the greatest danger of them all"—could match the danger posed by our attitude toward the problem. "It is our *thinking* that we must modify if we are to make and implement the decisions necessary to protect the world we live in," she said. Various interest groups had chosen sides and were quick to blame the crisis on others, but the real problem was how to get everyone working on the solution. While no society had been able to come up with a feasible way to end environmental contamination, it was her view that "the peoples of the world can be expected to husband the environment of the earth when they understood the facts of their interdependence and the irreplaceability of resources." The crisis can lead to a necessary transformation in man's thinking, to work with nature instead of trying to conquer it.

The environmental crisis is made all the more imperative by the population explosion. With the world's population at four billion and expected to double before the year 2000, the pressure on the frail environment is nearing the breaking point. For Mead, the situation was clear-cut: Without population control, it would be impossible to protect the environment. Mead advocated birth control not only as a right of individual women and couples, but as the only possible solution to the interrelated problems of energy shortages, pollution, hunger, and the economic development of the Third World. As a representative to the 1974 United Nations World Population Conference in Bucharest, Mead participated in the development of a "world plan of action" on population control. The plan rested on three pillars: First, it recognized that continued unrestricted population growth would eventually wipe out any social or economic gains made in developing countries and would further imperil the environment. Second, it assumed that consumption patterns would have to be changed. The United States, with only 6% of the world's population, would have to stop gobbling as much as half the world's resources. Finally, the Bucharest plan recognized that merely providing birth-control devices would not guarantee that people would use them. Desperate people would be prompted to have even more children, to increase the chances that one of their offspring would live. The only sure way to make birth control work, said Mead, was to create the conditions that would give people hope for a better life.

Mead saw the population explosion as both an individual and a group responsibility. "If we are to restore some kind of balance to the relationship between population and earth resources," she said, "we will have to find ways to shift human beings from the present retreat from individual responsibility to a recognition of just how creative and significant each individual can be." Population control, she said, depended not only on the dissemination of information and birth-control devices, but on developing a "new conception of the individual" in which each person seeks fulfillment not in breeding replicas of himself but in the nurturance of all human children everywhere and in "the realization of what each individual can contribute . . . to a world that desperately needs every ounce of creativity we can free for productive thought and social action." Population control was not solely the obligation of the poorer countries. To put the whole burden on them without doing something about population control in the industrialized countries not only smacked of racism to Mead, but was a policy without hope of success.

To Mead, population control and the fight against hunger were intimately tied. "We must balance our population so that every child that is born is well fed," she said. Her interest in nutrition was fired by her earliest South Seas expeditions, where she was forever recording the dietary habits of the peoples she studied. In 1939, President Roosevelt appointed her to a blue-ribbon panel looking at the suffering of the "third of a nation" that was ill-fed, ill-clothed, and ill-housed. During World War II she served as executive secretary of the Committee on Food Habits of the National Research Council and after the war held a number of positions with UNESCO and other international health agencies.

As an observer of food production and consumption patterns for more than three decades, Mead noted that almost all deficiency diseases in the United States had been wiped out during the war; by the 1950s the country's greatest nutritional problem was (and still is) overeating. Yet during the 1950s and 1960s a number of events— principally the rapid urbanization of poor families from the South into the cities of the North and the inability of the welfare system to deal with them—had combined to produce wide-scale hunger among the destitute. By the late 1960s, ten million Americans were malnourished, undernourished, or living on the edge of starvation. Even in the land of plenty, there was an America for the rich and (to recall Michael Harrington's phrase) "the other America" for the poor.

But if hunger in the United States was shocking, the situation was many times more horrifying in Asia, Africa, and Latin America. Here again, American consumption patterns figured into the relative distribution of resources between rich and poor. Because of the inefficiencies of converting plant protein into animal protein—it takes several pounds of grain to add one pound to a steer or chicken—Western society was consuming more than its fair share of world food resources. Children in Bangladesh and India were vying with American beef cattle for nutrients. "Children *do* eat grain," said Mead, "so as a result we now have human beings competing with animals for the same food, a situation which produces a very uncomfortable, and in the final analysis, a very unethical picture." Not even the much-heralded Green Revolution, with its miracle rices and wheat, could solve the problem: It might, according to Mead, "ameliorate the present situation," but it is no answer to the population explosion. The Green Revolution might even backfire, because it relies on petroleum-based pesticides and fertilizers that pollute the environment.

To alleviate hunger, then, Mead foresaw the need for a new world ethic. Speaking as a Christian, Mead recognized that man's duty to feed those less fortunate had been compromised in the past by the reality of scarcity. To feed others might mean starvation for oneself. Today, there is no such excuse. "We have the food," Mead said; it was a political and economic decision not to distribute it. "For the first time in history, we have the technical competence to feed all the hungry; failure to do so only highlights the extent to which man's relationship to the environment has emphasized exploitation, extraction, expediency, and inhumanity." As for Americans, Mead said, they must preserve an ethic that will not let people starve, if there is anything at all that can be done to prevent it. "The day that we are willing to kill people *now* so that others have a better life *later*," she said, "we will have instituted a process that is continually destructive."

We must, therefore, solve the immediate problems of deprivation, to save the children of today from the terrible effects of deficiency diseases in the early years for, as Mead noted, "What they [children] lose is lost for good." But it is also necessary to look at food production in the context of the protection of the environment. Husbandry of nature's resources must be linked to the production of man's sustenance. If we tolerate hunger today, Mead implored, "where are we going to get people who are going to worry about pollution or ugliness of the environment fifty years from now?" We must look upon the environment as the primary resource of man's dominion, and upon food as its principal product. "We must cherish our land, instead of mining it, so that food production is first related to those who need it; and we must not despoil the earth, contaminate, and pollute it in the interests of immediate gain." Or, as she put it in another context, "If we don't care about the children . . . that are starving [today], . . . why are we going to care about the environment of the future?"

These issues figured into the larger question of economic development. If, as Mead observed, people all over the world want modern medicine and health care, agricultural technologies, transportation, and communications, how could these benefits be made accessible without destroying a people's culture or environment? Could primitive societies move into the 20th century without disruption? And, given the stress on the earth's limited resources, could modern industrialization be achieved everywhere without population control?

As the world's preeminent anthropologist of cultural change, Mead had witnessed primitive societies skipping centuries of development in a few decades. She had observed this phenomenon first among the Manus, who washed the pig fat out of their hair one day and stepped across a boundary of thousands of years into the second half of the 20th century. On a 1967 visit to Tambunam, the Iatmul village she had first studied in 1938, Mead recorded an equally remarkable change. "Without self-consciousness," she says, a man tells her, "I will now sing the song we used to sing when the heads of the slain were lined up in the men's house." A few minutes later he tells Mead: "Yes, my youngest son is away at school. He is studying to be a doctor."

But the postwar glorification of modern technology frightened Mead. It was as if the world's industrialized countries took pride in the undeveloped countries' wanting Western technology. The wisdom of the day called for the developed nations to devote 1% of their gross national product to the industrialization of the world's poor nations, so that every nation-state could be modernized as quickly as possible. When Mead and other anthropologists objected on the grounds that industrialization should be congruent with the rest of the culture and should not tear people from their moorings, from established customs, from the wholeness of their culture, they were roundly criticized for being paternalistic and denying primitive peoples their natural "right" to modern technology. Once, during the war, she was attacked by a fellow anthropologist for suggesting that South Sea islanders not be supplied with bathtubs. "Anybody who has ever been on a Pacific island knows that what they do not need is a bathtub; they have the whole Pacific Ocean to bathe in every day," Mead said.

By the 1960s, after writing a technical manual for the World Federation for Mental Health entitled *Cultural Patterns and Technical Change,* Mead came to the dismaying conclusion that international aid efforts had bogged down. In Geneva, at the 1963 United Nations Conference on the Application of Science and Technology for the Benefit of Less Developed Areas, Mead bemoaned the fact that only one-fifth of the participants were from poor countries. Moreover, the optimistic postwar predictions of worldwide industrialization were quickly fading from memory. "By the mid-1960s it was clear that the simplistic dream in which the industrialized countries . . . would be able to spread their benefits to the entire world was not turning out as expected," she said. Industrialization, automation, commercialized agriculture, and related policies that once seemed "so promising" had to undergo "a terrible reevaluation."

Mead also doubted the validity of the presuppositions on which these policies were based: the belief that increased industrialization would automatically benefit undeveloped countries, without consideration of the possibly disastrous side effects—increased urbanization, uprooting of village life, decaying social order, and rising unemployment for those moved off the farms; the practice of treating certain basic occupations, such as farming and housing production, as industries (primarily for exportation or job production) instead of seeing them as ways to produce food and shelter; and the distinction made between production and consumption, as if people don't consume what is produced. Not enough was being done to determine how much and what kinds of technology were "appropriate," to use E. F. Schumacher's term, for various kinds of developing areas. "They do demand electricity, but the question is, how is that electricity to be generated, and need it be generated in the ways that it is being generated here?" asked Mead. She questioned sharply the motives of the industrialized countries in distributing aid to undeveloped countries. Writing in *Foreign Affairs*, she said, "The focus is not on hungry people, wherever they may be, but on underdeveloped countries." In other words, foreign aid programs were being used as political clubs to beat the proper ideology, whether capitalism or communism, into starving people—not, as the superpowers professed, for humanistic purposes.

But it was the deification of the gross national product that irked her the most. "Our present notion of just going up, and up, and up, and up with the GNP without considering all these other factors, is a linear notion that is self-defeating and is likely to set up all sorts of problems—and in the end disastrous restraints," she said. Our metaphors for describing industrial growth were, in Mead's view, "extraordinarily inappropriate." One, based on the physical sciences, assumed that conditions improve for some only at the expense of others; the other, based on biology, held that a nation's economy goes through states of development from birth to death, like a single organism, and that any decline in growth was a sign of impending disaster. In rejecting these comparisons, Mead said we need a new figure of speech that likens GNP to an ecological system, so that societies could achieve a proper balance among all their aspects. "What is needed is a kind of dynamic equilibrium which can become more and more diversified, richer, more elaborate and in which every person can have a qualitatively higher standard of living and a better way of life," she said. Increasing GNP without considering the effect on the quality of life, particularly such unquantifiable items as the cleanliness of the environment, was senseless. "We realize now that worldwide mechanization is wrong," she wrote in 1971. "It creates too much pollution. It's no longer viable." Instead of giving underdeveloped countries 1% of our GNP, we were actually exporting a portion of our pollution. Not that Mead was entirely against growth, or even in favor of placing limits on growth. She *was* for setting limits on materialism—on unbridled consumption and mindless technological expansion—and for establishing a better balance between population, resources, and technology. And she saw great potential for raising the quality of life for all peoples. "The technical skills and resources exist; no one in the world need be hungry, or cold, unclothed, uneducated or unmedicated," she said. "Standards can be set below which no people anywhere should be allowed to fall." She believed in progress, she added, only in terms of a higher quality of life, of "a world in which every child is wanted," and not merely in terms of the gross national product. The challenge is not raising the standard of living but altering the standard of living. The results of technology "have brought us to a place where, for the first time in human history, it is possible for one person's gain not to be somebody else's loss."

What, then, was Mead's solution to this complex array of problems? Is there any hope of finding a solution? For Mead the optimist, the greatest hope lay in the fact that there was so little time to solve the problem. "But just because the situation is so urgent," she said, "just because so many millions are so hungry, just because a pall of warning smog hangs over the great industrial cities, just because it is so urgent to find solutions we may hope that we will be impelled to find them." If there were more time, she said, we might do nothing.

To find solutions, it is necessary to be aware of past errors. The energy crisis first awakened the industrialized world to the impending disaster and underlined man's misconceptions about the environment. One-dimensional, one-shot approaches to solving problems would not work; instead, said Mead, we need a vision, "a frame of reference, a model of cherishing care for the earth and all human needs." That takes both long-range planning and the ability to engage in a sustained effort even grander in scale than the Manhattan Project or the moon flight.

In mankind's history, only war or some equally calamitous event has been sufficient to move masses of people to action. Today, with a *"totally* new picture," we need "something quite different from what we've ever asked from men before," said Mead. What were needed were people who so love their country and its future generations that they will be willing to make the kinds of sacrifices that people historically have made in war. For Americans, this is a novel challenge, because for the first time in history, the American people were being asked to defend themselves and everything they hold dear, *in cooperation* with all others on this planet, who share the same endangered air and oceans. "This time there is no enemy," said Mead, "there is only a common need."

The solution, then, lies in a new attitude about the earth. Man must learn to cherish the earth as fragile and delicate, yet sufficiently mutable to permit him to apply the wonders of science and technology to its salvation. But the plan cannot be piecemeal: It has to be looked at whole. Imagining the earth as if from space, she said, "I think that the tenderness that lies in seeing the earth as small and lonely and blue is probably one of the most valuable things that we have now."

Fortunately, the mechanism for such holistic, long-range planning is already at man's disposal—the computer. Through the development of elaborate computer models, such as those used in the so-called first Club of Rome report, it is possible to create reasonably accurate forecasts of world population, food supply, natural resources, air and water quality, and other indicators of the quality of life.* Although the Club of Rome report forecasted a bleak future (and some experts challenged its methods and findings), the point remains that man has the technical tools necessary to come to grips with the problems of the environment, energy, hunger, population control, and world economic development.

That does not mean we should stand around and wait for the computers to spew forth all the answers. There are many specific, immediate actions both nations and individuals can take. To combat hunger at the international level, Mead saw a need to develop food-related policies that would respect the traditional food patterns of people in developing countries (so as to avoid taboos and to conform to cultural preferences) and to change consumption patterns in the affluent countries to stop overnourishing people. Other international policies she supported, such as those advocated at the 1974 Rome Conference, include the development of world food banks to care for people hit by famine, and the need to transfer knowledge, skills, and working capital to countries that cannot feed their people. At the individual level, Mead suggested that Americans, the world's biggest consumers, eat at least one restricted meal a week, sending the money saved to an international aid group such as UNICEF to help feed the poor. She also recommended that Americans cut down on meat, avoid "extravagant and wasteful food habits," and pay more attention to nutrition.

As for population control, a "new climate of opinion" was,

*Donella H. Meadows, Dennis L. Meadows, Jørgen Randers, and William W. Behrens III, *The Limits to Growth* (New York: Universe Books, 1972).

according to Mead, apparent in the reforms advocated at the 1974 Bucharest Conference: the need to redesign birth-control techniques to fit conditions in each culture; the importance of improving social and economic conditions, particularly reducing the infant mortality rate and improving conditions for the elderly, so as to give people hope for a better life; and a greater emphasis on the significance of technological development in shaping population policy. The Rome Conference of 1974 showed the need for greater involvement of women in setting birth-control policies. At the national level, governments can influence population control by not subsidizing large families through tax policies, by providing information on birth-control methods, by conducting research on birth control and sex determination (so that people will not have "extra" children in the hope of getting one of the "right" gender), by offering counseling on negative genetic factors, and by easing the procedures for legal adoption. Moreover, governments should set a policy of putting less of a premium on universal parenthood as a goal of society. In fact, individuals and couples could be encouraged to consider such options as marriage with no children, or new arrangements in which adults would care for and nurture other people's children.

Finally, those concerned about the economic development of emerging countries can learn from Mead's own experience in Manus about what happens to a primitive culture that is suddenly modernized. When she returned to Peri in 1953, she told the Manus, "I have come back because of the great speed with which you have changed, and in order to find out more about how people change so that this knowledge can be used all over the world." From the Manus, Mead did indeed learn that not only is rapid change possible, but actually desirable. Instead of advocating slow, piecemeal changes for emerging cultures, said Mead, "we should advocate that a people who choose to practice a new technology or enter into drastically new kinds of economic relationships will do this more easily if they live in different houses, wear different clothes, and eat different, or differently cooked, food." Cultural transformations of the kind demanded by the increasing industrialization of the world should be conducted in broad strokes. Each human culture, she said, "like each language, is a whole, capable of accommodating within it the wide varieties of human temperament." Learning another culture is like learning a second language, and the easiest way to do that is to immerse oneself in the task.

Equally important, the Manus moved through the cultural change as a unit, never forgetting their past. Instead, they took their own modernization "in their own hands, redesigned their culture from top to bottom, asserted their full dignity as modern Manus," but never broke the tie with their past relationships. The whole transformation came from an old mesh of human relationships that was "rewoven into a new pattern from which no thread was missing."

The advanced countries of the West could take a lesson from the Manus. They, too, must see that the contamination of the atmosphere and oceans, the population explosion, famine, and the abuses of technological development are not isolated problems, but part of a complex web. Only by acknowledging the shared nature of these problems, said Mead, could we hope to solve them. Singling out her own countrymen, she said that it is vital for Americans to move forward into a new era "in which the entire nation is involved in a search for a new standard of living, a new quality of life, based on conservation not waste, on protection not destruction, on human values rather than built-in obsolescence and waste." But this sense of shared destiny must not be confined by national borders. "For the future," said Mead, "our one sustaining strength will be a sense of our common humanity." Rampant technological change and overpopulation have brought us terribly close to the brink—a point of great danger, yes, but of great opportunity as well. To Mead, the situation was not without spiritual implications: "For the first time we have the chance to bring about the world we have dreamt of, prayed for, and hoped for, throughout the whole of man's long journey to this day," she said. For the first time, the whole of mankind is at the edge of a precipice, and only common action can save it. By sharing in this apocalyptic vision, said Mead, people of all beliefs can be united in a search for a better tomorrow for all.

Can we find the solution in time? she asked. "That is both the question and the answer." With more time men might feel less compelled to work diligently *today* to prevent disaster. But the very magnitude of the task, said Mead, "may be used to reduce every human being to a cipher, or to ennoble each as a part of a whole larger than we have known before."

8
The Meaning of Community

A misty morning in June 1967: Margaret Mead, accompanied by her colleague Rhoda Métraux, is speeding up the Sepik River of New Guinea in a power boat. Her destination: Tambunam, the Iatmul village she had studied for eight months in 1938. Its people, once proud headhunters, now are limited to stalking the crocodile; and though the village had been bombed during the war and floods had washed away many of its yam gardens and coconut trees, Tambunam remains physically much the same as when Mead left it.

As she steps from the boat, Mead is approached by an old woman bearing a duck, which she gives to the visitor. After a few moments, the purpose of this ceremony becomes clear: Twenty-nine years before, Mead's husband, Gregory Bateson, had given the woman's husband a pearl shell. This is her first opportunity to return the courtesy.

Mead later recounted this story to make a point about the meaning of community. Real community, she said, is based on memory, on "shared experience over time, . . . continually revivified by comment, by reference, by telling the story over and over again." Among the Iatmul, as among other primitive peoples, memory persisted over five generations, from one's grandparents to one's grandchildren. Relationships were automatically determined by the kinship system. One could not help but be part of the community, for one was born into it.

This sense of community is lacking in most of the so-called civilized world, Mead noted. While in primitive cultures the family or tribe automatically creates a communal structure for the society, no such structural framework exists in the modern industrial or postindustrial society. Villages, towns, and cities are built around the fulfillment of needs—commerce, recreation, government, industry. Only as an afterthought do its residents concern themselves with the creation of a community, a place based on personal relationships grounded in memory. Cities, towns, and neighborhoods, therefore, are rarely communities in the sense Mead implied. Nor does housing, or other physical development, create a community, as the experience of suburban and new-town development shows.

It is not surprising that Mead would take a lifelong interest in cities. As an anthropologist, she was committed to the study of societies, hence civilization. Civilization depended on the establishment of cities (the Latin root "civitas" means city), where a small leisure class could be freed from the burden of daily labor to indulge in nonproductive activities, such as art, philosophy, culture, and science.

As an ethnologist working in the field, moreover, Mead was exposed to the rapid cultural change affecting primitive societies. She was used to villagers in New Guinea coming out of the Stone Age one moment and in the next starting to worry about crime, the creation of slums, and the migration of outsiders into their territory. Her work with UNESCO, the World Health Organization, and the World Federation for Mental Health also kept her abreast of the problems of cultural change and urbanization in the developing countries of the world. She also served as a consultant to the housing commission of New South Wales and participated in Habitat, the United Nations Conference on Human Settlements, held in Vancouver, British Columbia, in 1976.

In the 1960s Mead took part in the Delos Symposion, a kind of floating university sponsored by Constantinos Doxiadis, a Greek city planner and the founder of ekistics, the science of human settlements. For one week each summer, some thirty-five participants—of the caliber of British economist Barbara Ward, historian Arnold Toynbee, and engineer-inventor Buckminster Fuller—would cruise the Aegean aboard the *Semiramis,* skimming the islands of Skíathos, Thásos, Sámos, Rhodes, Santorin, and Míkonos, and anchoring always at Delos, the ancient center of the Athenian federation. Along the way, Doxiadis would lead his band of architects, planners, engineers, futurists, and thinkers in far-ranging discussions of ways to improve the quality of urban life. These voyages shaped much of Mead's thinking about the complex problems of cities and made her a thoroughgoing advocate of ekistics.

Mead's education in cities was shaped not only by these intellectual pursuits but by personal experience as well. As a child in Bucks County, Pennsylvania, she would visit New York to see her god-mother, Isabel Ely Lord, who taught at Pratt Institute in Brooklyn. When she transferred from DePauw University in Indiana to Barnard College in the fall of 1920 she became a true New Yorker. As a student, she quickly learned the ways of the city—how to catch the open-topped busses to get to the theater, where to spot the lovers in Riverside Park, how to sneak into the Forty-second Street Library, where students were not welcomed. She learned to soak in the joys and comforts of the city—poetry readings, the Turkish baths, *thé dansant* at the Astor Hotel—and to pay it back in turn by teaching Sunday school at St. Clement's Church in Hell's Kitchen, or by picketing with the garment workers in Times Square. For more than fifty years her office at the American Museum of Natural History was her only real, per-manent home. New York, she said, taught her how to nest in a gale.

She was less concerned with the physical structure of cities than with their social networks. Until recently, she pointed out, cities were established for defensive purposes, production, or the distribution of high-level services such as medicine and the arts. As a result of such technological advances as the telephone and television, the auto-mobile, and the computer, the traditional purpose of cities has largely been obviated. But that doesn't mean that cities are disappearing. Quite the contrary. In vast portions of the globe, people are abandoning the boredom and poverty of the countryside to settle in cities, where they have some hope of finding a place to live and something to eat. In that sense, the city continues to fulfill its function as a gathering place for people from wide and varied backgrounds.

But cities today are changing in a significant way. In the past, it was possible to distinguish between the city and the surrounding rural area. Today, the demarcation is unclear. Not only has the area between the city and the countryside been filled in with urban sprawl, but it is physically possible, thanks to the automobile, to move between city and countryside with relatively great speed. The result-ing urban structure is what Mead called "the city triumphant," where every necessity or whim—for food, people, art, culture, love, science, medical care—lay within a forty-five-minute drive. These urban structures are not merely larger versions of the traditional city, but a whole new kind of configuration, where one city more or less grows into the next, forming a continuous urban belt. (The areas from Boston to Washington and from San Francisco to San Diego are examples.) Jean Gottmann, the urbanologist, called such an urban structure "megalopolis."

The problems of megalopolis are necessarily linked to those of the big cities, said Mead. It is the cities that contain the slums, the huge concentrations of the poor. They segregate people into groups by superficial characteristics such as race, income, age, and social class. They are polluted. They are crime ridden and plagued by juvenile delinquency. They divorce children from nature, from experiences that will help them to understand their own bodies, and even from experiences that will help them use the full potential of the city. In addition, the city portions of megalopolis have proven unlivable for families with children, while the suburbs, which are supposed to be ideal for children, are "probably the most atrocious ekistical invention made in the history of the human race." The majority of people who live in megalopolis take little or no part in the cultural and intellectual life of the city that is its focal point. Furthermore, megalopolis is so diverse that it is practically impossible for all the competing interests to agree on what should be done for the greater good of the community.

Part of the blame for the lowly state of the cities must, in Mead's estimation, fall on those who build them—architects, planners, developers, and engineers. She told a conference of city planners in 1975 that once, in trying to decide whether to subscribe to a certain architecture magazine, she studied a few recent issues of the publication. What startled her—and presumably cost the magazine a subscriber—was that there were no people in any of the photographs, a clear sign to Mead that the designers of these buildings were more concerned about massaging their egos than about providing for the needs and comforts of the buildings' users.

Why have architects and planners failed in their designs for buildings and cities? Because, she said, they have divorced themselves from their clients and consequently have lost that unquantifiable but salient factor known as "human scale." She called the problem "designing at a distance," the attempt by building professionals to create structures for people they had never met or did not respect. "The whole country is full of teapots that won't pour, of light fixtures that don't work, of doors and windows that let out the heat and let in the cold," she said. The ignorance and lack of respect was exaggerated when the users differed in background, social class, or age from the designers, which explains in part why public housing almost always looks like a prison and why planners insist on isolating old people in "golden ghettos" for the elderly rich and high-rise slums for the elderly poor. "When buildings are built by people who wouldn't demean themselves by living there, the buildings are ugly," she said. This disrespect also explains why, in times gone by, servants' quarters were purposely kept menial, even though the architect could have made them much more elegant at no added cost. And because designers retained the image of the nuclear family as the ideal, they ignored whole segments of the population in designing housing: singles, divorced people, childless couples, and anyone else who didn't fit into the prescribed mold. Moreover, architects imposed design styles on their buildings that were often totally inappropriate to the climate of the region and the needs of the users. It was, in short, a question of attitude: Those responsible for constructing cities had not attained an understanding of and respect for the people they were designing for. The result: Buildings and cities that were unusable and unlivable.

The loss of human scale, said Mead, also led to another problem—the tendency of those responsible for building houses and cities to treat them as consumer items: so many housing units produced each year, creating so many jobs, contributing so many dollars to the economy. Nowhere in this equation is there mention of the nonproductive aspects of houses and cities, their contribution to the quality of life of the people who inhabit them. Instead, they are looked upon as items for sale, not homes that give people dignity and a greater sense of humanity. "Houses do a great deal more than house people," Mead noted. They contribute to the cognitive development of children by, for example, helping them distinguish differences between shapes. They also channel human relationships, permit or constrain freedom of choice, structure age and sex relationships, and pattern hierarchical or egalitarian forms of behavior. They are not just objects of consumption.

Mead was fully aware that creating new options for city dwellers, particularly those who traditionally had been ignored by city builders, would necessarily complicate urban life. She understood perfectly well that multiplying the number of options only made the problems geometrically more difficult to solve. She found no solace in simplistic solutions, such as banning high-rise buildings. High rises, she said, were not inherently damaging to the city dweller's psyche, as some urbanologists claim. (She herself lived in one for years.) In fact, they offered a convenient form of living for special groups of residents, such as wealthy couples with no children at home or elderly people who could "commute" by elevator to see their friends. High-rises could be made even more livable, she said, by providing a recreation room or common area on each floor, thus creating a space where residents could congregate and form relationships.* She was aware, too, that planners and others in city development were trying to solve these problems, not always successfully. "I understand from my friends the planners," she told an interviewer on a trip to Australia, "that if they were allowed to do what they wanted to do everything would be splendid, but they never have."

The question that truly intrigued Mead, however, was the distinction between the physical and social characteristics of cities. Most city dwellers, for example, call the place where they live their neighborhood. To the question "What do you like about your neighborhood?" most people refer to its cleanliness, the quality of the public schools, or the upkeep of the houses and streets. Most Americans, Mead lamented, worry more about the outward appearance of the physical components of the neighborhood than they do about the people who live there. Such neighborhoods rarely have a sense of community.

True neighborhoods, on the other hand, perform a number of valuable functions, according to Mead. They are places where basic physical and physiological needs are taken care of—the supply of food and water, sleep, and privacy. (But not always the latter: Mead recalled her experience in the Samoan village of Peri, where the only privacy afforded her was a blanket hung between her and the others living in the same hut.) Neighborhoods also perform the invaluable function of being the places where children are raised to become members of their society. A neighborhood supplies a continuity of

* A Columbia University psychologist recommends much the same thing in his book on the effect of density on urban dwellers. See Jonathan Freedman, *Crowding & Behavior: The Psychology of High-Density Living* (New York: Viking Press, 1975).

human relationships, where children in particular can learn to adapt to the needs and demands of their culture, while at the same time providing multisensory stimulation to achieve maximum use of their faculties and develop sensory discrimination—learning to distinguish a dog's walk from a person's, or how the weather affects one's environment. Among the most important characteristics of city neighborhoods are their qualities of strangeness and danger. While it is important for children to have places where they feel protected, Mead said, it is equally important that they be exposed to the unexpected so that they can learn to cope with dangerous situations— city traffic, for example. Without this ability to face strange and possibly dangerous situations, city children would quickly perish. Mead compared the situation to that of one tribe she was familiar with, where the people never learned to swim. When the nearby river changed course and cut its way through the middle of the village, the children who fell into the river of course drowned.

In 1942, while on the Committee on Food Habits of the National Research Council in Washington, Mead met Dr. Muriel Brown, a psychologist and prominent student of communities. At that point in their respective careers, Mead had (among other accomplishments) published *And Keep Your Powder Dry,* her study of American national character, while Brown had written two handbooks for community workers. It was apparent to them both that they shared an interest in defining the meaning of community, particularly in the context of American society. After the war, Mead pursued her work for UNESCO, the World Health Organization, and the World Federation for Mental Health on the effects of urbanization and cultural change in developing countries. Brown worked for various service organizations in Germany, Egypt, and Pakistan, and in 1951 published a book, *With Focus on Family Living,* a study of experimental community organizing projects in the United States. In 1966 they coauthored *The Wagon and the Star: A Study of American Community Initiative.*

The book, which derives its title from the phrase "Hitch your wagon to a star," brought together Mead's thoughts on American national character as applied to communities and Brown's experience working with community organizations. In it, the authors trace the development of community activism in the United States from its founding to the present, supplementing the text with case studies of successful community efforts: Tin Top, a little Texas town that rebuilt itself after disaster struck; Arlington, Virginia, where a small band of citizens helped reform local school politics; and such national organizations as the Parent Teachers Association. In each case, individual citizens spotted a problem, alerted their neighbors and other concerned individuals, and volunteered to solve the problem.

In essence, those are the distinguishing characteristics of American community action, Mead and Brown say in *The Wagon and the Star*. A community, in their view, is "a group of people who share a common concern and are doing something about it." Merely living in the same city neighborhood or rural town does not mold people into a community. They must be working together, usually on a voluntary basis, to try to make the place where they live better. One of the peculiar aspects of the American character, in fact, is this sense of individual responsibility for communal problems. It is the mark of the American's sense of responsibility that when something goes wrong in the community—when the schools don't teach children to read, or when the sewers constantly back up—the citizen presumes he personally can take action to get things put right. In other societies, people assume that only someone "in government," or with city hall, or otherwise in a position of power or authority can solve such problems. That anyone can, on his own initiative, seek to rectify some wrong or improve existing conditions is truly a foreign concept to non-Americans.

With this sense of individual responsibility for community problems comes another uniquely American quality: the sense of struggle. Mead and Brown found American community life to be characterized by "a special kind of group dynamics," in which the old order is challenged by the new. This tension creates a sense of constant movement, of action and interaction, give and take, not only in large urban centers but in smaller towns and villages as well.

And what of the city of the future? Looking forward to the year 2000, when most people on earth will be living in cities, Mead said, "The time has come when we must ask: How can the world of the future—a world of cities—be made a fit home for all mankind?" In the United States, cities have already become places to avoid because of the difficulty of raising children there, the poor quality of the public schools, the fear of crime, and the lack of open space. But the problems of cities extend worldwide. Addressing her fellow scientists in preparation for her participation in Habitat, the 1976 U.N. Conference on Human Settlements, Mead said that the 140 governments and 400 nongovernmental units represented in Vancouver had a momentous task before them. "As old cities decay before the onslaught of penniless millions . . . new cities, jerry-built and inhuman, spring up. . . . The pollution, poverty, and over-crowding in our cities . . . dramatize the contemporary problems of reconciling planning and freedom, human well-being, and the enhancement of profit, power, and prestige."

The cities of the future must, in Mead's estimation, be designed to accommodate new possibilities and new patterns. They must be built for change and dynamism. And they must be constructed in the context of the whole earth. Real planning for human settlements, as hoped for at the Habitat Conference, must be based not on antiseptic qualities—"cold and statistical" city planning, "distant and inhuman" population control, "sanitary" pollution control, and "miserly" resource conservation—but on planning for whole communities, as well as at the national and international level. Thus, planning must be conducted on a worldwide scale, using the technology at our fingertips, notably the computer, so as to avoid any further damage to the environment and particularly to the atmosphere.

Mead called her ideal city "the City of Man." To the City Triumphant, where every service and product is available to the resident, she would add the fundamental principles of democracy, making the good life equally accessible to the poor and downtrodden as well as to the leisure class, avoiding exploitation of the poor and minorities.

Creating the City of Man will necessitate a restructuring of megalopolis, replacing the current sprawl between urban centers with a series of small urban centers clustered around large cities. This would give people who might otherwise choose to settle in the large cities the option of finding the good life in the small towns and villages of their youth. Though small towns are popularly viewed as the places where dreams take shape, whereas big cities are the places where dreams are fulfilled, the small town is making a resurgence in popularity, notably for young families with children. Moreover, in purely physical terms, small towns and cities have a lot to offer—choice sites for industrial and commercial development, natural resources such as water, an existing population for a labor and sales market, and established institutions and networks, such as hospitals, trade associations, clubs, and public services. They can play a major role in the restructuring of megalopolis, according to Mead. Similarly, there is a role in this new structure for new towns, self-sufficient satellite cities linked to the big cities by high-speed transportation systems. Mead saw new towns as laboratories for the testing of new patterns of development and living. Though new towns could house only a small fraction of the population, they could be test sites for new ideas in city planning—new ways to bring a slum back to life, or bold experiments in transportation or the elimination of racial discrimination. But Mead found the new towns she inspected something of a disappointment. In New South Wales, where she served as a consultant to the housing commission, the new towns had failed to create communities, in Mead's definition of the term. The development of complex interrelationships among people had not occurred. Nor had new towns in the United States been able to create the kinds of "instant communities" that their founders so hoped for.

While small towns and new towns will contribute to the restructuring of megalopolis, it was to the big city that Mead turned as the primary instrument of change. The city will always remain, she said, as long as man has a need for contact with other humans—"rich, variegated, unexpected, easy, multidimensional human contacts in the flesh." Cities must be maintained as centers of interchange, where people with diverse backgrounds and experiences can meet and be intellectually stimulated. The young, in particular, need the vitality and excitement of the city to fulfill their desire for adventure, challenge, novelty, hope. At times the city will seem strange; indeed, there are times when city residents feel as if they are living in a fantasy world, as if a movie, and not real life, were being acted out in the streets. With so many people of different backgrounds crowded together, it is not surprising that reality and artifice get distorted in the minds of many city dwellers. In this respect, the city of today has become what Mead called the "confrontation point," a place of discovery, where new residents and particularly the young can engage in a wide variety of new and enriching experiences. Thus, the city will always remain what Mead referred to as "a crucible of human imagination."

The trend toward megalopolis, said Mead, is not inevitable: Urban structure can be changed, either by changes in human patterns, such as population growth or decline, or by direct intervention in the process of urban development. Mead recognized that any effort to change urban structures and to revitalize our cities would take initiative by citizens, beginning at the grass-roots and working up to regional, national, and even international levels. The day when planning for cities could be done in a vacuum, without consideration of the effects of future development on people and the environment, is long gone. That prospect makes planning for new urban structures even more difficult than in the past, but it also adds to the challenge.

9
Race, Science, and Culture

Margaret Mead's attitudes about race and social justice were shaped at an early age. As a young girl, she was reminded that her paternal grandfather, Giles F. Mead, had fought on the Union side in the Civil War; and when Margaret was ten years old the family moved to a Bucks County farmhouse that had been a station in the Underground Railroad. Her mother taught young Margaret to call the Negro woman who worked for them "Mrs." and instilled in her the necessity to show "tremendous care" for the poor and anyone who was different. It was her mother who opened young Margaret's eyes to the stark realities of racial abuse, when she informed the eleven-year-old girl that the wife of one of the ex-slaves living in town had been raped by a white man and that was why she had a half-white son. And it was Emily Fogg Mead who, through her own field of study of conditions among Italian-American immigrants (then considered an under-privileged "racial" group) in Hammonton, New Jersey, impressed upon Margaret the need for optimism in relations with those less fortunate. Through integration and education, Mead's mother be-lieved, even the most wretched immigrants could be brought into the American fold. Later, as a graduate student in psychology at Columbia, Mead retraced her mother's steps to conduct further research on the children of these same families.

Raised in what must be considered an upper-class family by

intellectual parents, by a mother who believed in social causes, in a small, rural town far from the maelstrom of racial turbulence to be found in the big cities, young Margaret was relieved of the day-to-day burden of addressing her thoughts about discrimination and class difference. In her own words, she was a girl who had "never questioned her privileged status but who [had] absorbed an ethic that is deeply critical of injustice in the world." Yet she herself did not taste the bitterness of meaningless discrimination until her freshman year at DePauw University, when she was rejected for membership in a sorority because she wore the wrong kind of dress to a rushing party. That experience soured her against any system that smacked of unequal opportunity or arbitrary disqualification due to intrinsic characteristics.

Mead's initiation into the full implications of discrimination came during her early anthropoligical expeditions. It was in New Guinea that she came to understand the true nature of the caste system, under which the "natives," the men of the bush, had to kowtow to "Europeans," as all whites were called. The maintenance of this formal relationship was a matter of life and death, particularly where women were concerned, as Mead learned when she was put in charge of a labor line with no other Europeans, man or woman, around to help her keep order. There were two hundred workers on the line, men who, while not technically slaves, had traded several years' indentured service for the privilege of working for the white man. The workers had to learn to act humbly, to speak deferentially, to call the European "Master." But the white person also had to keep up this front of white supremacy, or the whole house of cards would collapse. One slip, Mead knew, one betrayal of her own fear and uncertainty at being able to control these two hundred men, some of whom had been cannibals and all of whom were fierce fighting men, and she would be dead. And her death could lead only to retaliation by the government and the death of many of the men. Even though she was repulsed by it, Mead knew that she had to perpetuate the strict caste system.

Another lesson in the workings of the caste system came when she was alone in a remote village with only the women present, the men having left on an expedition. Some strange men came into the village and tried to sell her some worm-eaten beans. She refused to buy them, and shooed them away. After they had gone, she noticed a box of matches was missing from the table. This might seem a trifling matter, but under the caste system a white person could not show weakness by letting a thief go. Mead knew that she had to get that box of matches back or she would be killed, and with her half the village would be slaughtered in retaliation. So she drew up her courage and went storming after these fearsome men, unarmed and totally defenseless against them, and demanded the matches back in no uncertain terms. Meekly, one of them reached into his bag and drew out the matches. The village was saved! But the incident once again proved to Mead that the caste system was a life and death affair every single minute.

All this was brought home to Mead the first time she ever traveled in the South, in 1942. In the fashion customary to Northerners, she smiled politely at the porter—a Negro, of course—and then saw the look of unbridled terror in the poor man's face when he realized that a white woman was smiling at *him*. It was an experience that stayed with her all her life.

For Mead the anthropologist, the problem of racial discrimination had to be understood within the context of man's unique position in nature. Unlike other species, which can improve only through genetic changes, man alone among living creatures can, through his ability to learn and to articulate what he has learned, carry his improvements forward from generation to generation. Even human groups that have been isolated in some jungle or mountainous waste can be brought into the mainstream through the process of learning. It is also unique in nature that man's capacity to learn is interchangeable; that is, while one culture may be ascendant at a certain point in history, another (not necessarily descended from the first group) may come along and raise civilization to new heights.

What is less understood, and therefore less accepted, is the anthropologist's principle of the psychic unity of mankind, the knowledge that while there are several racial stocks, each remarkably different from the others, there is only one human species; and further, that within each racial stock, there is the capacity for producing individuals as gifted as those who have preceded them. Yet throughout history, either out of self-interest or ignorance, men have elevated one group or another to a position of superiority and at the same time denigrated others solely on the basis of some arbitrary characteristic such as skin color or physique. This is the very nature of prejudice—prejudgment, without regard to the facts. Once the line between the superior and the inferior group has been drawn, both groups believe it to exist in reality; worse still, both groups suffer because of it: the group thought inferior by actual physical or mental anguish, and the allegedly superior group by the moral pain suffered in denying full humanity to others. Mankind in general suffers as well under such circumstances, Mead noted, since any society that approves of slavery, caste, pogroms, or any such form of brutality has to be considered less than fully human.

Every culture passes along an understanding of certain basic differences, such as the difference in size between an adult and a child; instinctively, as well, children learn to distinguish—and even to fear—other superficial differences, such as skin or hair color, physique, or body hair. If children are exposed to only a few examples of people from outside their own culture, they tend to build up stereotypes based on the behavior of these isolated cases. To take a couple of blatant examples, the white child whose only experience with blacks is seeing a black man laid out drunk on a sidewalk and the black child whose only experience with whites is with a white policeman who harasses people in the neighborhood are going to have equally distorted images of other kinds of people. Unless efforts are made to expose children to a wide variety of people different from themselves, Mead said, they will be hard-pressed to understand that there is good and evil, indifference and warmth, in all groups of people, and that they should not prejudice their relations with people on the basis of isolated instances of behavior.

The method of educating children by pointing out differences is especially pronounced among American families, Mead noted. Since American society has no well-defined rank or caste system, each family positions itself in relation to other families or stereotyped groups. Children are taught to behave by comparing their own background to that of others: "Don't wipe your nose on your sleeve, only immigrants do that," a mother chides her son. Or she might say to her daughter, "Don't you want to dress up for the party like the Anderson girl?" the Andersons being the local family of background. (Mead herself was not immune to this kind of training. In a singular comment of prescience, her grandmother told her, "Come and get your hair combed. You look like the wild man of Borneo!") This system of comparison becomes the basis for teaching children the differences necessary to enter their culture. Discrimination, in this sense, is a process of acculturation learned in the home.

As an anthropologist, Mead wanted to know more about the question of race and intelligence than the process by which children learn to discriminate by group. Was there any scientific evidence to prove that the innate intelligence of one race was greater or less than any other? And if not, what other factors might account for any observed differences in intellectual performance between the races?

These were hardly new questions. But the development of standardized tests for the measurement of intelligence in the early part of the 20th century set the stage for further refinement of the classic debate over innate ability. Although the original purpose of intelligence tests was to provide a means for school administrators to be able to identify children with below-normal learning ability (that is, children whose IQ's were well below 100) so that those children could be given special training, IQ tests came to have a much wider use. Scientists began to make correlations between IQ scores and given characteristics of the tested population—whether the children came from the cities or the farms, whether they were native-born or foreign-born and, for the latter, whether English was their first language or one learned since coming to America. During her graduate years at Columbia, Mead studied the Italian-American community of Hammonton, New Jersey, to compare the IQ scores of those children who spoke Italian at home versus those who spoke English at home. The results, compiled in her master's thesis in psychology, "Intelligence Tests of Italian and American Children," showed a significant difference for the English-speaking children over the Italian-speaking children. These results indicated to Mead that cultural factors, not differences in innate ability, accounted for differences in measured intelligence among various groups of people.

In the United States, the debate over the innate intelligence of minority groups was given impetus by the U.S. Supreme Court's 1954 decision in the *Brown* case. Although the court resolved the legal issue of separate but equal schools for blacks, it left open the question of whether some cultural factor was responsible for the relatively poor showing of blacks on intelligence tests, or whether the perceived difference was due to a deficiency in innate ability. The court could not be expected to adjudicate such an issue. That was up to society, particularly those in the sciences of human development.

Mead was prepared neither temperamentally nor intellectually to believe any assertions about the innate mental inferiority of any group, particularly blacks. She was upset by what she called "the barrage of pseudoscientific statements" about the people socially classified as Negro, and set out to do something about it. Thus she found herself in the forefront of efforts by the scientific community to put the matter to rest. In 1962, the American Anthropological Association requested the American Association for the Advancement of Science to investigate whether any new evidence had been found to prove blacks innately inferior. According to Mead, the AAAS's appointee, Dr. L. C. Dunn, reported no new evidence to contradict the basic anthropological position of comparable mental capacity for all large human populations. Dunn's findings were reaffirmed in 1963 by the AAAS Committee on Science in the Promotion of Human Welfare. Later that year, the committee's statement came under attack from Drs. Henry E. Garrett and Wesley C. George, as well as Carleton Putnam, who, according to Mead, used familiar but still weak arguments—one of them being that fire was discovered by African man fifty thousand years after its discovery by European man—as evidence of the innate mental inferiority of American Negroes. Mead and other scientists saw the need for the relationship between race and intelligence to be clarified.

In 1965, in the midst of this controversy, Mead and Dr. Theodosius Dobzhansky, a professor of biology and genetics at Rockefeller University in New York, were appointed cochairmen of a committee on the biological and social aspects of race by the Scientists' Institute for Public Information. SIPI was founded in 1958 by a coalition of scientific groups whose members sought to provide accurate information to the public on policy matters of a scientific nature, particularly those related to the environment. The organization's guiding force was Barry Commoner, the Washington University ecologist, whose St. Louis Committee for Environmental Information was the prototype for SIPI. Among its first members were Mead and Dobzhansky. The SIPI committee's work culminated on December 30, 1966, with the holding of a nine-hour forum at the AAAS meeting. The seminar brought together some of the best minds in the field and resulted in the publication of *Science and the Concept of Race,* edited by Mead, Dobzhansky, Ethel Tobach, and Robert E. Light.

Mead, assuming her customary role as the organizer and collator of ideas, stated that the SIPI forum reaffirmed earlier findings that no relationship between race and intelligence had been proven. As she herself had stated earlier, differences in intellectual achievement could be attributed only to cultural factors—education and social conditions. "The most powerful influence on man's mental achievement," she said in 1963, and reaffirmed many times later, "appears to be his culture."

But other commentators asserted that race had some relationship to lower scores by blacks on intelligence tests. A year after the publication of *Science and the Concept of Race*, Arthur Jensen, in a *Harvard Educational Review* article, "How Much Can We Boost IQ and Scholastic Achievement?", reopened the whole debate, questioning not only the lower achievement scores by blacks but also the efficacy of learning enhancement programs such as Head Start.

The answer, for Mead at least, lay in a fundamental misunderstanding of the term "race" as applied to American Negroes. In the period from 1870 to 1920, said Mead, many of the immigrant groups who came to the United States were identified as separate "races," and the relatively low IQ scores they registered were given as evidence of their inferiority. Later, as these groups were assimilated into the culture, their IQ scores proved as normal as the rest of the population's, indicating once again the cultural bias of such measurements. The stumbling block proved to be the idea that different groups of immigrants constituted separate races, when of course they were actually part of the much larger stock of Caucasian humans. In scientific terms, Mead noted, a race is defined by an "intricate statistical patterning" of traits, such as blood type. By these criteria, the American Negro, whose African ancestry might be as minute as one thirty-second (or less) of the individual's heritage (and rarely constituted his full genetic composition) was clearly an extraordinarily diversified group—hardly a race in the scientific sense of a "closed Mendelian population," as might be the case with such isolated groups as African desert dwellers, Alaskan Eskimos, or the inhabitants of Pitcairn Island. The American Negro, by contrast, contained many different ancestors. Mead called attention to the findings of Dr. Bentley Glass, Distinguished Professor of Biology at the State University of New York in Stony Brook, who showed that the typical Negro from Baltimore averages only 70% African descent. To ignore the other constituents of the American Negro's ancestry and place him in one "race" on the basis of his African ancestry alone seemed to Mead the grossest misuse of scientific evidence. To Mead, the term "Negro" (or "black") was a political and social designation used to define a group of people within the American culture, but it was not a scientific classification. Hence the argument of "racial inferiority" was built on a faulty theoretical foundation.

Mead saw the need for constant vigilance against any effort to link race and intelligence. She was timely in her call to arms, for no sooner did Jensen publish his article than he was joined by William Shockley, Richard Herrnstein, and others. It was the scientist's duty, Mead proclaimed, to bring the tools of science to bear on this problem, for the good of mankind. To do less—to allow statements about differences in innate intelligence to go unchallenged—would only increase the price "in human suffering, loss of human potential, and ethical damage that this country is paying."

One of Mead's more unusual contributions to the debate over race was her collaboration with the novelist and essayist James Baldwin on *A Rap on Race*. The story behind the book is interesting. A young black editor, Art Aveilhe, approached Mead with the idea of doing a book about race. "You have something different to say and people might listen," he told Mead. They talked about the idea for a while, and Mead recounted her experience with the caste system in New Guinea. "I won't write a book on race unless I can write it together with a black man," she said. "We need both parts of the picture. White women, who must never forget, and black men, who must never aspire, together have carried the burden of preventing violence. Together we know." A few days later, Aveilhe called. Would she be interested in taping a conversation with James Baldwin that would be edited and made into a book? After rereading several of Baldwin's books, Mead agreed.

On the weekend of August 25, 26, and 27, 1970, Mead and Baldwin met for their "rap on race." The taping lasted about seven-and-a-half hours. At times the conversation rambled, and the two got sidetracked frequently.

Judged on the whole, however, the conversation proved constructive. Each participant brought his special insight to the subject— Baldwin, the novelist's eye for image and detail and his fiery passion as a black American who chose self-exile in France over inferior treatment in the United States; and Mead, the scientist's concern for method and accuracy, and the anthropologist's broad understanding of the influence of culture.

The most enlightening point of contention in *A Rap on Race* is the disagreement that erupted between Mead and Baldwin over the question of the white American's guilt for the suffering of blacks. At first, Baldwin accepted Mead's point that one cannot be held accountable for past events in which one had no part. One is responsible only for what is happening and what can happen.

On the second day, however, Baldwin eagerly returned to the theme of white guilt. Somehow, in assessing guilt, he said, we had to account for time. He asked Mead if she did not agree that what we call history may be a way of avoiding responsibility for what has happened, or is happening, in time. No, said Mead, we can't be blamed for what we can't control. But, said Baldwin, one does have to accept "the history which created you"—one's ancestry, genealogy, heritage. "And if you don't accept it, you cannot atone," he said. To Mead, however, the idea that people today were responsible for the actions of generations past was completely repugnant.

And there lay the crux of the argument: Baldwin pressing for his vision, demanding that history, rather than being viewed as a way of avoiding responsibility over time, be seen as the instrument of atonement; and Mead, just as steadfastly, saying, "I will *not* accept any guilt for what anybody else did. I *will* accept guilt for what I did myself." To Mead's way of thinking, Baldwin was advocating a position comparable to the Russian Orthodox view of guilt—"If one man suffers, then we are all guilty." But to her, guilt by association did not hold. "Everybody's suffering is mine but not everybody's murdering and that is a very different point," she said. Responsibility, for the actions of both whites and blacks, she reiterated, lies in the present and in the future, not in the past.

Despite the bitterness over race in the United States, Mead told Baldwin, something is working to bring not only order and rectitude, but human value and goodness, to race relations. She called it a "moral force." It is represented by the likes of Martin Luther King, Jr., by the black children who risked their lives to integrate the Southern schools, and even by the white policemen in Chicago who reentered the black ghetto in the hope of working with the community toward some solution of its problems, even though a fellow officer had just been killed by a sniper's bullet. Their courage in the face of danger had to imply the presence of something terribly powerful, said Mead. "We have to postulate a moral force at work *on both sides* to explain that courage," she said.

What, then, could be done to harness this "moral force" and ease race relations in the United States? The task before Americans, said Mead, is to reconcile belief in equality with the tremendous diversity of the population. To say that all men are created equal need not imply that they are all the same. What it does mean is that each person should be extended full dignity and full respect for his rights as a unique human being, including full respect for his *differences* from the stereotype or the mainstream. Yet while acknowledging cultural differences and respecting political and religious differences (and teaching children to value diversity in others), we must ignore race. Mead was emphatic about this point. Ignore race, absolutely! she said. Lumping people together by race without accounting for cultural influences, such as poor education, can only stagnate relationships among the many groups that comprise America. "We will succeed only to the extent that we can bring ourselves to treat all individuals *as* individuals," not as members of racial or ethnic groups, she said. Our diversity must be acknowledged, said Mead, but that which unites us—our humanity—must be kept uppermost in our minds.

Any program for easing race relations in the United States, she went on, must recognize certain realities: first, that historical conditions have resulted in the creation of large groups of individuals of mixed descent; that grouping and segregating these individuals has damaged them socially; and, finally, that such a pattern of isolation leads to conditions that are "ethically unbearable, economically disastrous, and politically damaging."

Mead was less sanguine about the specifics of such a program. In 1966, the Committee for Economic Development, a nonprofit public affairs group in New York City, asked her to prepare a paper on "Equality Goals and Urban Progress." Today, more than a decade after the paper was written, her arguments seem naive; her recommendations, weak and diffuse. Among her proposals were finding incentives to attract the best lawyers, doctors, architects, and other professionals to work in the ghetto; encouraging active efforts to find "qualified Negroes" to fill important jobs, while at the same time refusing to grant blacks token recognition for inferior performance; and discouraging the racial typing of jobs. These are all certainly worthwhile recommendations, just as her proposal that city governments raise the standards of sanitation and safety in ghetto areas seems reasonable. Yet these suggestions hardly cut to the core of the problem, and they likewise fail to recognize the full political consequences, particularly the majority reaction. On school desegregation, Mead called busing (in another context) a "desperate measure" that should be corrected by some other means. What other means? Mead suggests building good schools with high-caliber faculties in areas where they might encourage residential integration so that no child, black or white, would have to be overburdened by busing—a nice thought, but politically unsophisticated. In any case, she told the Committee for Economic Development, the controversy could be abated somewhat if everyone agreed that no child should be bused to an inferior school, and if all the schools were improved—again, hardly a feasible program for action. In the context of the time, however, with the nation's cities bracing for a new wave of destruction each summer, and with the worst rioting still to come following the assassination of Dr. Martin Luther King, Jr., Mead can hardly be blamed for not having all the answers.

In the absence of specific programs, however, Mead did offer both a broad political agenda and a useful philosophical approach that could stand us in good stead today. The political agenda hinges on the need to meld the causes of integration and ethnic power by means of three mutually-supportive mechanisms. The first of these is to seek integration within those special groups where it seems most immediately viable—medical doctors, scientists, poets, and musicians, for example. The second point is the advocacy of political "black power" within the ghettos, in this case making skin color the basis for community organizing, much as the white immigrant groups of previous decades used ethnic origin as the basis for political unity. Finally, Mead's proposal calls for new social and economic development in the Old South, so that conditions in what historically has been the most economically depressed part of the country could be improved for both blacks and whites.*

The philosophical part of her program is premised on the need for a new ethic that eschews the concept of the inherent inferiority of any large group of people; rather, it presumes that all men are capable of learning. It assumes Mead's "moral force" to be at work, so that both the privileged and the underdog are working together to improve race relations. Finally, we must get the message out, beginning with the children, whom Mead called "our most fertile field" for sowing the

---

*The economic development of the Sunbelt already is taking the Old South in that direction.

seed of improved race relations. Only by stressing the principle that no one should face discrimination because of some racial or ethnic trait will we be able to imbue this principle in the coming generations. Only then can all children, black, white, red, brown, and yellow, be free to realize their full potential as human beings. "It is the state of our beliefs, individually and collectively, on which the creation of an open society depends," said Mead. Without a change in beliefs—a change that Mead thought could be brought about only with the addition of scientific knowledge—the potential for improving race relations in America is dim.

Mead will not be remembered as an activist, leading the picket lines and building the civil rights movement. But her scientific contribution to the discussion of race and intelligence cannot be forgotten. Her intimate knowledge of other peoples, vastly different from ourselves, made it possible for Mead to see the larger scheme of things, the psychic unity of mankind upon which the whole concept of racial equality rests. By educating the American public to the fact that culture, not inherent characteristics, is the dominant factor in intellectual achievement (and, as a result, economic and social achievement), she was able, in her own way, to break down some of the walls of prejudice.

In the foreword to the 1958 edition of Ruth Benedict's *Race, Science and Politics*, Mead said of her friend and mentor: "She left her own scientific labors . . . to go out into public places, to write, to speak, to sit all day on committees and in conferences, that the people of the United States might learn to treat all other men as members of the human race." That statement might as easily have been made of Margaret Mead herself.

10
A Faith for Today

It may come as a surprise that Margaret Mead was a deeply religious person. One expects cynicism from intellectuals, especially scientists, yet Mead never allowed her belief in the mystery and wonder of science to cloud her faith in God. Instead, she joined these twin faiths together to form a religious and ethical system for the postwar world. She called it a "20th-century faith."

Mead's religious development can, like so many of the turning points of her life, be laid in great part to serendipity. When the family lived in Swarthmore, she tried the Quaker meeting, but her father mocked her for it. She was allowed to attend various religious services with the immigrant maids who kept house for the Mead family, but none of these took hold. Her mother had given up on Unitarianism, and Grandmother Mead likewise had fallen away from the Methodist church. It was not until she was eleven years old that young Margaret found her true religion. The family was living in Buckingham at the time, and the local Episcopal minister and his daughter came to visit. Margaret decided to give the Episcopal church a try and "almost at once" found its rituals to be the form of religious expression for which she had been seeking. "I had not been looking for something to believe in," she said, "for it seemed to me that a relationship to God should be based not on what you believe, but what you felt."

After World War II, Mead began to translate these religious

"feelings" into a coherent set of principles. Upon returning to the United States from England in 1945, she began to ask how it would be possible to build a world order based on peace and mutual under-standing among peoples, when the world was so hopelessly divided by culture, religion, and politics. Even with two societies as closely linked as England and the United States, the difference in outlook was vast. The British saw themselves as the junior partners of God, caring for the world's garden in the hope of making it flourish. In contrast, Americans saw the world as theirs to make over—and as the explosion at Hiroshima would shortly prove, they had the absolute power to do it. This attitude was encapsulated in the joke about the engineer and the minister. They are looking at the gargantuan dam the engineer is building—a dam that will flood the whole countryside. "Yes," says the engineer, "it's just as God would have built it, if He'd had the money."

Mead admonished her countrymen for their hubris. It was impera-tive, she said, to reconcile the awesome power the Bomb held with the humility necessary to bring world order. That reconciliation could be achieved in only three ways: by refusing to associate with people of other cultures, by destroying any other culture that refused to conform to America's dictates, or by capitalizing on the diversity of cultures to make the world anew. This last choice would take true humility, Mead acknowledged, yet it was the only way to safeguard the future.

Over the course of the next three decades, Mead propounded her 20th-century faith, a religious and moral system that at once took in the terrible destructive power of the Bomb and the fantastic accom-plishment of the moon voyage, the horror of widespread famine and the miracle of the Green Revolution. For it was Mead's belief that science and religion could—indeed, must—work hand in hand to solve man's problems: to feed the hungry, shelter the homeless, clothe the naked, and heal the sick. In the postwar world, man could truly be his brother's keeper because for the first time technology made it possible to feed not just the people down the block, or in one's town, or even in one's own country, but the whole world. "One of the terrible things at present is the sense of futility and frustration and rage that we can now feed people—on a large scale not just a personal scale—we can carry out the admonitions of Christianity and we're not doing it." The technology existed; the moral will to carry it out did not. And for the first time, we could be certain that "the brotherhood of man" was not only a religious and moral wish but a scientific fact. Every corner of the world had been explored, and science had confirmed that mankind was indeed a single species.

But technology is a two-edged sword, Mead warned. Speaking before the World Conference on Church and Society in Geneva in 1966, she emphasized that technology may seem a miracle to a people who have never before seen television; to us, trapped in smog-filled cities, fearful of the next nuclear accident, worrying over the cancer-causing agents in our food, technology seems the harbinger of Armageddon. It is wrong, however, to blame science—the pursuit of knowledge—for all the evil effects of technology, just as it would be wrong to blame Christianity for the evils of Christians. Instead, man's goal in the postwar period must be to bring science and religion together. "With knowledge and no faith, we may well see a world destroyed," Mead told the Geneva conference. "With faith and no knowledge, we may still see a world destroyed. With faith and knowledge bound together, we can hope to cherish and protect the lives of the men and the life of the world." She believed that only a religious system "with science at its very core" could guide us into the future.

But religious principles had to be applied at an international scale. "Is it Christian to insist that it is nobler to minister to the individual sufferer than to use technology to wipe out the disease from which that individual is suffering?" Mead asked. The greatest sin for modern man, she said, is to have the knowledge necessary to help *all* his brothers and then fail to use it. This, she said, is the task of the Christian community today, "to learn to combine the command to love our neighbors as ourselves with finding out who our neighbors are, knowing all that is known about them, and knowing all that can be known about carrying out the Christian command."

To begin this awesome task, those who were serious about adopting a 20th-century faith should support the cause of world order, international law, and worldwide institutions. They should encourage the development of food banks to prevent famine and the removal of restrictions on the use of contraceptives to control population growth. They should support interim measures to bridge the gap between rich nations and poor and should encourage equality of opportunity for all races and socially dependent groups. They should be in the forefront of the environmental movement.

To attempt to reach these goals, however, could put organized religion in a dilemma. In terms of culture, Mead pointed out, religion has a dual role. Its conservative role is to be one of the major elements that forms the world view for the culture and helps provide a common way of life for the members of the society. Its dynamic role calls for religion to alleviate the stagnation of the culture. Thus, the conservative function of religion would include the continuation and propagation of church ritual, while the dynamic function might take in social work on behalf of the poor—functions, incidentally, that could and often did occur simultaneously. The difficulty came in achieving balance between the two roles. In a 1962 lecture at the historic Arlington Street Church in Boston, Mead criticized what she called the liberal church (in particular, the Unitarian church) for its "non-egalitarianism" in ignoring the poor. The liberal church must make an extra effort, she said, to shed its elitism and reach out to the underprivileged at its door. Yet it was possible for the clergy to go overboard on the social action side and forget the ministerial role. That is one reason why so many young people fell away from organized religion in the 1960s—not because of lack of belief on their part, but simply because of the failure of the churches to provide a deeply religious experience. The result, said Mead, was "ferment, uncertainty, and . . . impotence" in the church.

The new religious ethic of Mead's 20th-century faith arose from an understanding of the unity of the human spirit. Only through a sense of obligation to all mankind could a new world order be built. One means that Mead espoused for unifying all the peoples of the world was the cultivation of a world language—a second language, not a primary language, and a natural language accessible to the human tongue, not an invented one like Esperanto. It had to be written and easily transliterated into other scripts, and it had to have a large number of people who already spoke it, to act as teachers and translators. It could *not* be the language of a major political power or a language associated with any religion or ideology, for that would only serve to cause dissension among the major powers and most likely wipe out the lesser languages. It could be supplemented with glyphs—universal symbols for such expressions as "potable water," "right turn," and "lodging." Curiously, Mead was never able to come up with just the right world language. For a while she toyed with Malay, but the political ramifications with Indonesia interfered. The last suggestion she was known to make was Armenian. If it is hard to imagine four billion people learning Armenian as a second language, that reservation alone should indicate that Mead's proposal never enjoyed popular support.

If her proposal for a world language failed to catch on, her belief in the need for a shared vision—or a shared problem—that would join mankind did merit consideration. Today, that unifying element is the shared atmosphere. The threat to the atmosphere from radiation and pollution, she told students at Yale's Battell Chapel one Sunday in 1972, could be the means to bring mankind together, "a possible means of affirming the brotherhood of man." Repeating this point at the 1975 United Nations Temple of Understanding, a summit meeting of religious leaders representing 2,700,000,000 people, Mead saw the need for a common faith and a unity of spirit based on the terrifying threat of world destruction and "a dawning consciousness that survival of the smallest human group and survival of all humankind are joined."

The first step in the creation of this new world order, then, is "the recognition that peace no longer is an unattainable ideal but a necessary condition of continued existence." Mankind must look to a future in which every culture and every person is respected and cherished, she said; for if we chose to churn up ancient rivalries and demean our fellow man we might well witness the destruction of the world. Reiterating her theme of the unity of science and religion, she affirmed her hope in a 20th-century faith. "Faith and architectural principles erected our great temples and cathedrals," she said. "Faith and the human sciences are needed to erect a social order in which the children of our enemies will be protected as surely as our own children, so that all will be safe."

Mead put her construct of a 20th-century faith to work in her writings, speeches, and personal appearances, offering her counsel on the moral issues of the day. One of her special talents was the ability to take a contemporary ethical dilemma and examine it carefully for what it might have to say about higher philosophical and religious principles. Some time after a plane crashed in South America and the survivors admitted eating the flesh of their dead companions, Mead was asked by a *Redbook* reader what she thought of this seeming act of cannibalism. Her answer was typical of her approach to these thorny moral dilemmas. She explained the facts of the case briefly but meticulously, emphasizing that the survivors, faced with certain death by starvation (they had heard radio broadcasts that the rescue effort had been abandoned), devised strict rules as to what they were about to do. No one would eat the flesh of a relative; the flesh was to be cut into small pieces; and each night they would pray together. Later, after being rescued, they compared the experience of their communion with the human body to the eucharistic sacrament of the church. This, said Mead, is what saved them, for "the capacity of the survivors to interpret their act symbolically protected them from the fear of murder and the horror of cannibalism." She called it "an example of how faith and the power of deeply accepted ritual can mitigate the terror and horror of an otherwise unbearable situation in such a way as to protect the humanity of the participants."

It was this unique capacity to tie her scientific work—in this case, her personal experience with cannibals—to present-day moral issues that raised Mead's counsel to such a high level. In her *Redbook* columns, her articles in other women's magazines, and commencement speeches and talks before hundreds of social gatherings, she came to grips with many of the major issues of the postwar era, as the following summary indicates:

Birth control. Mead was an early and vocal proponent of birth control, not only as a means to give women greater individual freedom, but also to limit population on a global scale. She recognized the conflicts, of course: Catholicism pitted against more liberal religions; industrialized (but less populated) Western nations versus the underdeveloped and overpopulated countries of the Third World; the rising tide of nationalism and the desire of new nation-states to increase in size and influence. Spiritually, she recognized the need to "adapt the tenets of earlier ages to the exigencies of the modern world."

In a sense birth control is an issue that outpaced Mead's advocacy, thanks to the development of the Pill. But the Pill brought with it a new set of problems. On the personal level, it left the onus on the woman—an increased risk of stroke, hormonal disorders, and other medical complications. Mead wanted men to share more of the responsibility for birth control; instead, she said, the Pill probably had increased the incidence of venereal disease and made men more irresponsible in matters of contraception.

At the international level, Mead saw population control as imperative, given the limitations on the earth's resources. The ability—or, in the context of some societies, obligation—to bear children had to be balanced, Mead said, against the right to be well-born. As she put it, "Society must be persuaded that issuing fewer invitations to the next generation—one way of thinking about the postponement of births— will make certain that all of those invited will have a better time."

Abortion. "It's an incredibly brutal, lazy, cruel way of handling life," Mead said of abortion. "I feel it is unlikely that any woman is not harmed either psychologically or physically by an abortion. It's an abominable method of birth control."

Despite these sentiments, Mead was a long-time critic of restrictions on abortion. In 1963, she called for reform of all abortion laws because they imposed the ethical value of one group (primarily Roman Catholics and conservative Protestants) on all women. At that time, she favored changing the laws so that women would be given optimal medical care (including abortions, if necessary) so as to protect themselves and prevent the birth of children with defects. Taking a swipe at the anti-abortionists, she said, "We will be a better country when each religious group can trust its members to obey the dictates of their own religious faith without assistance from the legal structure of the country."

In later years, she called for outright repeal of abortion laws. It was impossible, she concluded, to legislate morality in a society as diverse as ours. First one group had been able to impose its will on the rest of society; by the late 1960s, another group demanding reform or repeal of abortion laws was ready to force everyone else to conform to its view. No matter which group "won," said Mead, some women (and to some extent some men) were bound to feel that their rights had been trampled upon. By getting rid of *all* laws restricting abortion, said Mead, the members of each group would be free to follow their own consciences: Catholic hospitals would be free to forbid abortions, for example, while public hospitals could give abortions under strict regulation from the medical community.

It was equally necessary to recognize the drastic societal factors that impinged on the abortion issue. For the first time in human history, Mead said, mankind need no longer concern itself with reproduction for the sake of numbers; today, the quality of life is the prime consideration, thus leaving us free, as Mead put it, "at least to discuss the possibility of not giving birth this week to every little human soul beating against the windows of life." Yet the issue had been made all the more complex by the drastic increase in abortions due to liberalization of the laws. The psychiatric profession was growing concerned about the psychological effects of abortion on some women, ranging from indifference to severe trauma. All this made Mead come to the realization that "reliance on abortion is at best a poor solution." Although she felt certain that abortion was more than justified in cases of rape, where the life of the mother was threatened, or when the fetus was abnormal, she still found it a perplexing situation. Abortion, she said, "no matter how phrased, is too close to the edge of taking life to fit into a world view in which all life is regarded as valuable."

In January 1973, the U.S. Supreme Court in its landmark ruling prohibited the states from denying a woman an abortion during early pregnancy. In commenting on the decision, Mead said it ratified the need for a humane and constructive policy to minimize abortions. Such a program would include a wide range of options: research on how American women were reacting to the experience of abortion; restrictions on the misleading advertisements of abortion "mills," and the creation of model clinics that would provide for a whole range of family services, not just abortions; and research on new and better methods of birth control for men as well as women. Mead also foresaw the need to develop workable national guidelines for abortion legislation, so that the states would not be permitted to erode the Supreme Court ruling (thereby, incidentally, predicting the Hyde amendment, by which Congress eliminated funds for abortions for welfare recipients). Finally, Mead called for a recognition of a new philosophy that having a child is a considered choice, not a necessity or obligation, and that to recognize that choice is in itself a responsibility that will cause people to give greater consideration to the consequences of abortion. Mead hoped this would reduce the need for abortions in the future.

Sexual mores. Mead was opposed to laws that imposed the standards of one segment of society on everyone else. She advocated the repeal of laws against homosexuals and recommended that bisexuality be recognized as a normal form of human behavior. These positions were taken on the basis of her belief in individual freedom of choice and the necessity to protect personal dignity. Curiously, Mead opposed the legalization of prostitution. She said prostitution exploited both the women and their customers, but it was the prostitutes alone who suffered the barbarity and cruelty of the anti-prostitution laws. These laws should be repealed as being discriminatory, she said, and new measures—to protect minors, to shield the unwilling from solicitation, and to save young girls from exploitation—should be enacted.

The right to die. As an anthropologist, Mead had studied and actually observed the rituals of death in a number of primitive cultures, and thus had a unique perspective on death in our own society. Among primitive peoples, and in Western society until this century, it was impossible to sustain the life of an old or injured person. Mead herself remembered as a young woman seeing such an old person "lying inert, perfectly cared for, sapping the family strength." Coming from the perspective of her profession, and in comparing the most primitive and the more advanced societies, Mead said that the good society makes it possible for the person himself to decide how and when he will die; but no society could be called good that forces death on the weak, the sick, or the unproductive. As for herself, she said, "I myself would wish to live as long as I could be a thinking and communicating person; I would not want to live as an uncommunicating body." Her standard: irreversible brain death, not heart beat and respiration.

As with her position on abortion, she favored the repeal of all laws placing any restrictions on the right of the individual to choose death with dignity. The burden of the choice had to rest primarily with the person himself, preferably through the means of a so-called living will made while he was mentally and physically sound. To place the burden on doctors and nurses, however, was unfair in Mead's opinion, since the medical profession must be committed to the maintenance of life. At one time, she suggested that some sort of board composed of persons with medical training (but not physicians or other medical practitioners) be created to evaluate specific situations, but she never fully fleshed out the idea.

What about euthanasia? She once called it "a horrible idea," since it begrudged those in need the care that a morally correct society should provide. Later, she modified her position somewhat to take in the person who, while not in need of life-supporting mechanisms, nonetheless faces a life of pain, senility, or other personality distortions, and inevitable death. Such an individual, Mead said, should have the right to ask "release from the suffering ahead." Said Mead, "I believe it is the right of an individual to choose not to endure destructive suffering that can only end in death," provided that such a choice is made within an ethical framework committed to the value of human life.

The legalization of drugs. To Mead the ethnologist, drugs were mood-altering substances that had been used throughout human history to soothe nerves, reduce anxiety, and provide a greater sense of conviviality at important ceremonies. Cultures have over-accepted drugs (as in the case of American Indian tribes newly introduced to alcohol); violently avoided them (as in the case of the Balinese, who reject liquor except under such extreme circumstances, like having to handle the dead); and used them in a complex and regulated way (as in the case of the use of wine in holy rituals or the prescription of small amounts of alcohol or drugs to the sick).

What concerned Mead was the puritanical and moralistic tone of America's drug laws, laws which she felt could lead only to more, not less, crime. Like Prohibition, today's "dangerous, illogical and inhumane" restrictions unnecessarily added to the crime problem. This was especially true in the case of marijuana, which Mead felt should not be placed in the same class as heroin.

As for specific reforms, Mead began with the decriminalization of the possession of marijuana—not necessarily its legalization, however, a point on which she felt grossly misunderstood. She did suggest that drugs be regulated and legalized to the extent that addicts be given or sold drugs at reasonable prices, under strict medical care, so as to be able to free themselves from addiction and the crimes associated with addiction. She also favored laws permitting young addicts to seek professional help without consulting their parents.

Civil disobedience. The act of defying a law that one believes to be evil or contrary to a higher law is "a highly moral piece of work." Civil disobedience is not a matter of taking the law into one's own hands, said Mead, as would be the case of the robbery victim who shoots his assailant without warning or quarter. Mead was also aware that, in a society as complex and diverse as ours, the possibility of the law violating individual conscience was almost inevitable. During the years of protest of the Vietnam war she approved of conscientious objection (even selective conscientious objection, when the war was not one of national survival) and draft-card burning, provided the person making the act of civil disobedience was willing to take the penalty. She chastised those who fled the United States, saying they should have stayed and worked for reform, and she doubted the sincerity of those who demanded amnesty for their acts. No matter what the particular circumstances, however, Mead believed that the principle of civil disobedience had to be acknowledged, for it was at times the only way that change could be effected. It remained, she said, "one of the strongest weapons in the arsenal of justice."

"The dangerous, Godless brain." In 1957 Mead and Rhoda Métraux surveyed 35,000 students in 118 high schools across the United States to determine the students' image of the scientist. Although the responses were partly favorable—for instance, scientists were praised for their single-minded devotion to their subject—the students' impression of the typical scientist was overwhelmingly negative. The average scientist was thought to be nothing short of a demonic, atheistic power, a dangerous, Godless brain whose machinations surely would lead to the destruction of the world.

These findings naturally disturbed Mead, not simply because this popular misconception often had a direct effect on scientific research (such as budget cuts for basic research), but because she herself had worked for years to inject humanistic values into the sciences. She was among the leaders of the movement within scientific circles to question the growing power of scientists in the postwar period, particularly their burgeoning role in political and military decision-making; and she was among the first to demand greater public access to the storehouse of knowledge kept under strict lock and key by scientists, so that the average citizen could play an equally informed role in the great scientific debates of our time—the effects of nuclear radiation, the use of insecticides and food additives, the control of the weather by artificial means, the continued reliance on fossil fuels, and the possibility of the artificial creation of human life itself.

Yet Mead, ever the consummate scientist, feared that research might be shackled with too many controls. She was opposed to placing limits on genetic research, to take one particularly thorny issue, even though she once compared genetic engineering to "human beings playing God" and called it "a dangerous thing to do." With regard to the debate over the costs of the space program, she came out on the side of further research, all the way to the moon. "People have always said that it would be better to stay home and till your own cabbage patch," she wrote at the time of the manned moon landing in 1969. "I think that if people don't follow the potentialities of movement and change, they're likely to wither and die." Although she once called the space program a "quasi-military, international sports event," she still felt it possible to combine it with a search for the solution to our earthbound problems. What is lacking, she said, is "only the will and the imagination."

It was Mead's belief that science itself, the actual pursuit of knowledge, was at best a neutral force; certainly it was not a kind of black magic, as some of its detractors said. The issue really was the *application* of scientific research—not whether research on poisonous gases should be conducted (for who knew what results, good or evil, might result?), but whether the deadly gas so produced should be used for evil purposes. This last point cannot and should not be decided by scientists alone. Instead, said Mead, we should work toward "new canons of responsibility" in the application of scientific findings, whereby both the scientific community, with its technical knowledge, and the general public, which is directly affected by these matters, will be involved in the decision-making. The scientist's job is to provide the information, but the final choice must be left to the public. Only in that way can we create "a climate of opinion, a sense of the role of the scientist as the responsible expression of a new civilization, a civilization to which disciplined self-awareness is the very breath of life."

In the postwar period, scientific progress has grown at an exponential rate, and with it the problem of directing the application of scientific findings to beneficial ends. The counterweight to the ever-burgeoning power of the scientific community, said Mead, is an informed public. But it is the task of the responsible scientist—the one who is concerned about directing scientific progress toward human welfare—to keep the public informed, so that the citizenry, and not some collection of "godless brains," would be making the political choices necessary to guide science to its proper goal, the betterment of humankind.

It would be injudicious—and inaccurate—to say that Mead had the right answer for every moral problem. For example, she advocated a daily period of silent prayer in the public schools "in which each child could pray as his parents had taught him to," thus ignoring the First Amendment right of nonbelievers to be free from such pressures by the state. (She also approved the idea of a constitutional amendment to permit prayer in the schools.) She favored denying the American Nazi

Party a permit to march in the predominantly Jewish village of Skokie, Illinois, because of the probable violence that would erupt between the two factions, failing to consider what such an abridgment of free speech and the right to assemble would mean to others. She opposed capital punishment, yet one wonders how she would have justified any lesser sentence for, say, John Wayne Gacy, the mass murderer who preyed on teen-age boys and buried his victims in the walls and basement of his home.

But these are minor failings. In a lifetime of writing, Mead brought considerable intelligence and humanity to the discussion of religious and moral issues. As we face an uncertain future, a 20th-century faith seems almost a necessity.

11
Last Rites

On the morning of November 15, 1978, as I was about to catch a plane to New York to do some research for this book, I heard the news that Margaret Mead had died of cancer at the age of seventy-six. I was not shocked to hear of her death. I knew she had canceled her entire summer's schedule of travel and lectures, something only grave illness could have forced her to do. But apparently only a small circle of intimates knew she had cancer. She wanted to be able to keep working, unmolested, as long as possible, and did so until just a few days before her death.

As I sat on the plane that morning, I thought about how much of a sacrifice Mead had made for me earlier that year. I had asked for her cooperation in writing a biography that would complete what *Blackberry Winter* had begun. At first, she openly opposed the idea, saying she preferred to do it herself. After an exchange of letters and phone calls, however, she changed her mind and suggested a meeting in Chicago. She would give me a few hours between flights on her way to the Menninger Clinic in Topeka, where she was to give her annual lectures.

Although Mead had been pleasant enough on the phone, I didn't know what to expect of her in person. One of my friends said, "I hear she's quite a terror." A prominent journalist whom I met referred to Mead as a "bitch," although she wouldn't elaborate on why Mead deserved such an appellation. When the fateful day arrived, however, my anxiety proved wholly unfounded. After greeting Mead at the plane, I took her to a small conference room at the airport hotel, where I proceeded down a list of items on the agenda I had prepared. She listened to my monologue for ten or fifteen minutes, then held up her hand and motioned me to stop. "What's your rush?" she asked. "Don't you want to talk?" I managed to calm down, and we talked. Mead wanted to know about my family, my career. Her questions were generous and warm; she was truly like a grandmother. When we got into politics, though, the sharpness of her mind became apparent. She asked me if I thought the American Nazi party should be allowed to march into the largely Jewish suburb of Skokie, Illinois—the big headline in the local newspapers that week. I replied that, as distasteful as these neo-Nazis were, they too were guaranteed the right of peaceable assembly and free speech. She argued against allowing them to march, saying it would be an invitation to violence; but I got the impression that she was really working out her ideas for a speech or article and was testing me for local color. In any case, after two hours of arguing with Mead, I felt as though my brain had been picked clean. I had heard of her remarkable ability to stimulate others to perform at higher than normal levels; now I had seen firsthand how she did it. By the time I walked her to the plane, I was exhausted, while Mead looked energetic enough to walk to Topeka.

She was dead before the year ended. Two days after Mead died, I attended the memorial service for her at Columbia University. St. Paul's Chapel was full well before the service was to begin, despite the heavy rains outside, but I managed to squeeze into a seat. The woman next to me, a widow in her sixties, whispered to me that she lived near the university and had attended many of Mead's lectures at Columbia and at the Museum of Natural History. "She made things very different for us, you know," the woman said, and I was about to ask her whom she meant by "us" (women? the elderly? Americans? parents? grandparents?—all had been touched by Mead's genius) when the organ sounded Bach's Prelude in B Minor.

In his homily, the university's Episcopal chaplain, the Reverend William Starr, praised Mead for her "exquisite mixture of scientific rigor and determined faith," the combination of "knowledge joined to action" that had informed her life. Three themes, he said, ran through her work: her sense of a shared humanity; her commitment to the family as the fundamental structure of society; and her confidence in the future, which enabled her to bridge generations and speak with empathy to young and old alike. I thought about what Mead herself had said, that she had had just enough hardship—the loss of an infant sister, the prospect of never having children, the many miscarriages— "just enough frost on the blackberries to make good fruit, but not enough to kill them."

Despite the hardships, Mead managed to put together a body of work whose depth and dimension should not be underestimated— some forty books, hundreds and hundreds of essays, reviews, speeches, lectures, and book prefaces, plus dozens of films, tapes, and radio and television programs. From that great mass of published work, it is of course easy to find specific points or arguments on which to disagree with her. For example, Mead's proposal for compulsory national service still merits careful consideration, but the idea of including college students in the program (and paying them to go to college, no less!) is almost laughable. As for her anthropoligical studies, here, too, it is possible to quibble with some of her more broad-stroked conclusions. The coincidence of her stumbling on the Arapesh, Mundugumor, and Tchambuli in the way she did was amazing, if not fantastic, and one must wonder whether she saw only what she wanted to see. (On the other hand, Reo Fortune, who was with her during those field trips, never disputed her findings, nor has any other scholar produced conclusive evidence to contradict her.) Certainly there was more than a little professional jealousy among her fellow scientists arising from her enormous popularity with the press and public. At times, though, she was simply too glib, and it is easy to sympathize with anthropologist Marvin Harris's assessment that "the courage of one's convictions is a blessing with which Mead has been liberally endowed."

Still, what a record! It is no exaggeration to say that had she published only her work on Oceanic cultures, Mead would still have to be classified in the highest ranks of social science and anthropology. Add to those seminal works her writings on education, science, religion, ecology, feminism, and so on, and it is clear that Mead was a major force in the shaping of 20th-century thought on a wide variety of topics.

Her personal life was also perfectly integrated with her work. She inspired others by her own example, not just in the simple things she did, such as keeping her own name after marriage (which is now the fashion for the "aware" woman), but in the substantive aspects of her life and work as well. Her daring and courage in venturing halfway around the world proved inspirational to countless numbers of young people, particularly women, many of whom took up anthropology because they had read one of her books and had been thrilled by her adventurous spirit.

She was more than a brilliant exception, more than a token female in a man's world. She liked being a woman and wanted more than anything to be a mother, a goal she achieved relatively late in life and only after much suffering and torment. To women, therefore, Mead was accessible simply because, having faced the trials of pregnancy and childbirth, she too was just another mother. She could speak with credibility to women (and to any men who cared to listen) about the problems of rearing children and running a family, without the hint of bitterness one hears in the voices of so many of those in the forefront of the women's movement. She carried her message in thoughtful essays and books, and in the way she lived her own life.

Her most important contribution, however, was her ability to assimilate information from a wide range of fields, process the facts, and somehow create a whole new viewpoint. As a self-appointed spokesman on a broad range of social issues, Mead possessed an uncanny ability to provide a sense of direction and purpose toward the solution of seemingly insuperable problems—population control, world hunger, environmental decay, poverty, the disintegration of the family, and on and on. She was able to see the relationships between things as no other commentator in the postwar period has done; she was the kind of integrative thinker who could put social and political problems in sharp perspective, with an understanding of the importance of culture as her intellectual foundation. Moreover—and this was the key to her success with the public—she could communicate her findings in plain English, heightened by precise and accurate imagery—the "rare weaving of the concrete and the abstract," as Wilton S. Dillon once put it.

She will be remembered most of all for her optimism. She simply could not be discouraged by the horrid events of the day, no matter how depressing they seemed. Twenty-five years after the war, when the great hopes of scientists and humanists of ridding the world of hunger, spreading the benefits of industrialization to the Third World, and achieving peace in our time and for all times—even when these dreams had been all but dashed, Mead saw hope for the future. Human ingenuity, imagination, and faith in life itself, she said, would enable mankind to reconcile the "terrible powers of destruction" and the "almost limitless powers of construction" that science has placed in man's hands. "I am optimistic by nature," she said. "I'm glad that I am alive. I am glad that I am living at this particular very difficult, very dangerous, and very crucial period in human history."

Her friend and former student, Jean Houston, once asked Mead for her own epitaph. Mead wrote, "She lived long enough to be of some use." * That assessment is of course too modest. For the better part of this century, hers was a strong, clear voice of reason in a world filled with babblings and false utterances. Who today is filling her role as analyst, commentator, and (in the best sense of the word) popularizer of those topics crucial to the survival of mankind? Sad to say, no one. With the death of Margaret Mead, the world lost not only a great humanist, but one of its preeminent philosopher-scientists.

---

* Her actual tombstone reads: TO CHERISH THE LIFE OF THE WORLD.

Notes to Chapters

1. Principal sources for this chapter include *Blackberry Winter: My Earlier Years* and *World Enough: Rethinking the Future* (with Ken Heyman); the chapter on Mead in Rae Goodell's *Visible Scientists* (Boston: Little, Brown, 1977); the foreword to *Aspects of the Present* by Rhoda Métraux; and Alice Marriott and Carol Rachlin, "Margaret Mead: A Woman of Science," *1968 Science Year: The World Science Annual* (Chicago: Field Enterprises Educational Corp., 1968), pp. 405–19. Among the periodical sources are: David Dempsey, "The Mead and Her Message," *The New York Times Magazine,* April 23, 1970, pp. 23ff.; Mary Ellin Barrett, "Margaret Mead: First of the Libbies," *Cosmopolitan,* September 1972, pp. 160–65; Gail Sheehy, "Why Can't a Woman Be More Like Margaret Mead?" *New York,* August 8, 1973, pp. 39–47; Joan Wixen, "I've Always Been a Woman . . . I've Never Been an Imitation Man," *The Sunday News Magazine,* Detroit, June 22, 1975, pp. 12–13ff.; Tom Burke, "Margaret Mead: Portrait of an American Original," *Cosmopolitan,* September 1977, pp. 180ff.; and Jean Houston, "Special Report: Margaret Mead at 75," *Saturday Review,* February 5, 1977, pp. 6ff., and "The Mind of Margaret Mead," *Quest/77,* July/August 1977, pp. 22–26ff.

2. The principal source for the section on Mead's early life is *Blackberry Winter.* The analysis of her anthropological expeditions is based on *Coming of Age in Samoa, Growing Up in New Guinea, Sex and Temperament in Three Primitive Societies, Male and Female, Balinese Character: A Photographic Analysis* (with Gregory Bateson), *New Lives for Old, Continuities in Cultural Evolution, Letters from the Field 1925–1975,* and "Apprenticeship under Boas," in Walter Goldschmidt (ed.), *The Anthropology of Franz Boas* (Memoirs of the American Anthropological Association, 89) (Menasha, Wisc.: American Anthropological Association, 1959), pp. 29–45. The quotation on field work is from an interview by William Mitchell, in James Nelson (ed.), *Wisdom for Our Time* (New York: Norton, 1961), pp. 65–75.

3. Besides *And Keep Your Powder Dry, Soviet Attitudes Toward Authority,* and *The Study of Culture at a Distance* (edited with Rhoda Métraux), Mead's major writings on national character include: "The Importance of National Cultures," in Arthur S. Hoffman (ed.), *International Communication and the New Diplomacy* (Bloomington, Ind., and London: Indiana University Press, 1968), pp. 89–105; "National Character and the Science of Anthropology," in Seymour M. Lipset and Leo Lowenthal (eds.), *Culture and Social Order: The Work of David Riesman Reviewed* (New York: Free Press, 1961), pp. 15–26; "The Study of National Character," in Daniel Lerner and Harold D. Lasswell (eds.), *The Policy Sciences: Recent Developments in Scope and Method* (Stanford, Calif.: Stanford University Press, 1951), pp. 70–84; "National Character," in A. L. Kroeber (ed.), *Anthropology Today: An Encyclopedic Inventory* (Chicago: University of Chicago Press, 1953), pp. 642–67; and "The Idea of National Character," in Roger L. Shinn (ed.), *The Search for Identity: Essays on the American Character* (New York: Harper and Row, 1964), pp. 15–27.

4. Mead's major works on the family include *Blackberry Winter, Male and Female,* and *Family* (with Ken Heyman). Many of her best articles on the family appeared in *Redbook Magazine,* notably: "Why Americans Must Limit Their Families," August 1963, pp. 30, 32; "Apprenticeship for Marriage: A Startling Proposal," October 1963, pp. 14, 16; "More About Limiting Large Families," January 1964, pp. 14, 20; "Margaret Mead Answers . . . ," June 1966, pp. 28, 30; "Marriage in Two Steps," July 1966, pp. 48–49ff.; "A Continuing Dialogue on Marriage," May 1968, pp. 44ff.; "Double Talk about Divorce," May 1968, pp. 47–48ff.; "Can the Family Survive?" September 1970, pp. 52ff.; "New Designs for Family Living," October 1970, pp. 22ff.; "A New Understanding of Childhood," January 1972, pp. 49, 54; "A Redbook Dialogue" (with Benjamin Spock), April 1972, pp. 80–81ff.; "Trial Parenthood," June 1973, pp. 26ff.; "Too Many Divorces, Too Soon," February 1974, pp. 72, 74; and "Divorce Insurance: A New Idea," March 1974, pp. 38, 41.

The section on the generation gap and the elderly is based on *Culture and Commitment* and the following: "The Wider Significance of the Columbia Upheaval," Fall 1968, pp. 5–8, and "Margaret Mead Replies," in "The Columbia Upheaval: an Exchange," Winter 1968, pp. 41–42, both in *Columbia Forum;* "An Anthropologist Looks at the Generation Gap," in *A Search for the Meaning of the Generation Gap: A Symposium* (San Diego: Department of Education, 1969), pp. 31–41; "The Generation Gap," *Science,* Vol. 164, No. 3876 (April 1969), p. 135; and "Grandparents as Educators," *Teachers College Record,* Vol. 76, No. 2 (December 1974), pp. 240–49.

Other significant publications on the family include: "Broken Homes," *The Nation,* February 27, 1929, pp. 253–55; "The Family in the Future," in Ruth Nanda Anshen (ed.), *Beyond Victory* (New York: Harcourt, Brace, 1943), pp. 66–87; "Can America Afford Families?" *Look,* December 12, 1944, p. 90; "What Is Happening to the American Family?" *Journal of Social Casework,* Vol. 28, No. 9 (November 1947), pp. 323–30; "The Contemporary American Family as an Anthropologist Sees It," *American Journal of Sociology,* Vol. 53, No. 6 (May 1948), pp. 453–59; "Modern Marriage: The Danger Point," *The*

Nation, October 31, 1953, pp. 348–50; "Family Life Is Changing," in Sidonie Matsner Gruenberg (ed.), *Encyclopedia of Child Care and Guidance* (New York: Doubleday, 1954), pp. 675–82; "Why Large Families Are Fashionable Today," *pb, The Pocket Book Magazine* No. 2 (New York: Pocket Books, 1955), pp. 31–43; "Future Family," *Transaction,* September 1971, pp. 50–53; "The Future of the Family," *Barnard Alumnae,* Winter 1971, pp. 6–8; "Statement," in *American Families: Trends and Pressures, 1973. Hearings Before the Subcommittee on Children and Youth of the Committee on Labor and Public Welfare, U.S. Senate, 93rd Congress, September 24–26, 1973* (Washington, D.C.: U.S. Government Printing Office, 1974), pp. 121–33; "The Family—How to Protect It" (Los Angeles: Women's Division, Reiss-Davis Child Study Center, April 28, 1975); and "From Popping the Question to Popping the Pill," *McCall's,* April 1976, pp. 66, 260.

5. The opening quotation is from an interview with R. David Heileman in the Berea, Ohio, *News Sun,* October 19, 1972. The material on Mead's own education is based on *Blackberry Winter* and "What I Think I Have Learned about Education, 1923–1973," *Education,* Vol. 94, No. 4 (April–May 1974), pp. 289–406. "Why Is Education Obsolete?" appeared in the *Harvard Business Review,* Vol. 36, No. 6 (November–December 1958), pp. 23–36ff.

Other sources of Mead's views on education include: "Our Education Emphases in Primitive Perspective," *American Journal of Sociology,* Vol. 48, No. 6 (May 1943), pp. 633–39; "High School of the Future," *California Journal of Secondary Education,* Vol. 35 (October 1960), pp. 360–69; "Continuing Our Present System Isn't Enough," in *Today and Tomorrow: Three Essays on Adult Education in the Future* (Chicago: Center for the Study of Liberal Education for Adults, 1961), pp. 34–38; "The Early Adolescent in Today's American Culture and Implications for Education," *Junior High School Newsletter,* Vol. 1, No. 2 (February 1963), pp. 1–6; "Some Considerations about Educational Issues in the 1970s," in *Needs of Elementary and Secondary Education for the Seventies: A Compendium of Policy Papers, Compiled by the General Subcommittee on Education of the Committee on Education and Labor, U.S. House of Representatives, 91st Congress, First Session, March 1970* (Washington, D.C.: U.S. Government Printing Office, 1970), pp. 588–91; and "Are Any School Administrators Listening?" *Nation's Schools,* Vol. 87, No. 6 (June 1971), pp. 41–45.

Her best work on the progressive movement is "Toward an Educational Protocracy," *New York University Education Quarterly,* Vol. 6, No. 3 (Spring 1975), pp. 2–7. On world literacy, see "Fundamental Education and Cultural Values," in *Fundamental Education: Common Ground for All Peoples: Report of a Special Committee to the Preparatory Commission of UNESCO, Paris, 1946* (New York: Macmillan, 1947), pp. 150–78; and "The Contemporary Challenge to Education," in *Fundamental and Adult Education* (UNESCO), Vol. 12, No. 3 (1960), pp. 105–12.

6. Among Mead's most important essays on women is her introduction and epilogue to *American Women* (edited with Frances B. Kaplan) and "Styles of American Womanhood through 200 Years of History," in *The American*

Revolution: A Continuing Commitment (Washington, D.C.: Library of Congress, 1976), pp. 55–65.

Other writings on feminism include: "Woman: Position in Society: Primitive," in Edwin R. A. Seligman and Alvin Johnson (eds.), *Encyclopedia of the Social Sciences* (New York: Macmillan, 1935), Vol. 15, pp. 439–42; "Women's Social Position," *Journal of Educational Sociology*, Vol. 17, No. 8 (April 1944), pp. 453–62; "What Women Want," *Fortune*, December 1946, pp. 172–75ff.; "American Man in a Woman's World," *The New York Times Magazine*, February 10, 1957, pp. 11ff.; "The Secret of Completeness," in "Symposium: The Gift of Self," *Good Housekeeping*, May 1960, pp. 72ff.; "What Makes Women Unhappy?" *Chatelaine*, March 1960, pp. 25ff.; "Do We Undervalue Full-Time Wives?" *Redbook Magazine*, November 1963, pp. 22ff.; "Where American Women Are Now," *Vogue*, May 1969, pp. 176–78ff.; "Women: A Time for Change," *Redbook Magazine*, March 1970, pp. 60ff.; "Women: A House Divided," *Redbook Magazine*, May 1970, pp. 55, 59; "What Shall We Tell Our Children?" *Redbook Magazine*, June, 1970, pp. 35ff.; "Two Possible Answers for Women," *The Tablet*, Vol. 65, No. 46 (December 1972), p. 2M; "On Freud's View of Female Psychology," in Jean Strouse (ed.), *Women and Analysis* (New York: Grossman/Viking, 1974), pp. 95–106; "Liberation Liberates," *World Health* (WHO), January 1975, p. 33; "Needed: Full Partnership for Women," *Saturday Review*, June 14, 1975, pp. 26–27; "Margaret Mead Answers . . . ," *Redbook Magazine*, August 1975, pp. 10, 14; and "Diversity of Choice for Women" (Wellington, N.Z.: United Women's Convention, 1976), pp. 12ff.

7. Mead's work on the environment is scattered about in numerous articles, notably "Challenges and Perils in Our Global Future" (Palm Beach, Fla.: Proceedings of the 95th Annual Proprietary Association Meeting, April 3–7, 1976), pp. 68–79. Her work on cultural change is best summarized in *New Lives for Old, Cultural Patterns and Technical Change*, and *World Enough*, with additional commentary in *Letters from the Field 1925–1975*.

For shorter writings, the reader is referred to: "The Underdeveloped and the Overdeveloped," *Foreign Affairs*, Vol. 41, No. 1 (October 1962), pp. 78–89; "Population: "The Need for an Ethic," *Journal of Medical Education*, Vol. 44, No. 11 (November 1969), pp. 682–83; "The Changing Significance of Food," *American Scientist*, Vol. 58, No. 2 (March 1970), 176–81; "Earth People," in *Earth Day—The Beginning* (New York: Bantam Books, 1970), pp. 222–23; "Economic Growth and the Quality of Life," in *Scenario for Growth: International Two-Day Discourse at Toronto on Economic and Social Growth, May 27–28, 1970* (Toronto: Toronto Stock Exchange, 1970), pp. 18–42; "Hunger, Food and the Environment," in *Hunger: A Scientists' Institute for Public Information Workbook* (New York: Scientists' Institute for Public Information, 1970), pp. 3–5; "Women and Our Plundered Planet," *Redbook Magazine*, April 1970, pp. 57ff.; "Human Values and the Concept of an Optimal Level of Population," in S. Fred Singer (ed.), *Is There an Optimum Level of Population?* (New York: McGraw-Hill, 1971), pp. 298–301; "Dialogue on the Future" (with Roger Shinn), *Youth*, Vol. 23, No. 12 (December 1972), pp. 2–15; "Prospects for World Harmony,"

Indian and Foreign Review, Vol. 11, No. 5, (December 1973), pp. 20–21; "Changing Perspectives on Modernization," in John J. Poggie, Jr., and Robert N. Lynch (eds.), *Rethinking Modernization: Anthropological Perspectives* (Westport, Conn. and London: Greenwood Press, 1974), pp. 21–36; "World Population: World Responsibility," *Science*, Vol. 185, No. 4157 (September 1974), p. 1113; "The Energy Crisis—Why Our World Will Never Again Be the Same," *Redbook Magazine*, April 1974, pp. 54ff.; "Pollution: The Need to Think Clearly about Clear Water," *Redbook Magazine*, May 1974, pp. 38ff.; "The Relationship of the Bucharest Seminar to the Main Currents at the United Nations Conference on Population," in *The Cultural Consequences of Population Change: Report on a Seminar Held in Bucharest, Romania, August 14–17, 1974* (Washington, D.C.: The Center for the Study of Man, Smithsonian Institution, 1975), pp. 1–6; and "How Can We Help the World's Hungry People?" *Redbook Magazine*, March 1975, pp. 49–50ff.

8. The reference to Jean Gottmann is to his *Megalopolis* (New York: Twentieth Century Fund, 1961). Mead devoted lengthy sections of *World Enough: Rethinking the Future* to cities. Her major articles on the subject include: "Values for Urban Living," *Annals of the American Academy of Political and Social Science*, Vol. 314 (November 1957), pp. 10–14; "1. The City as a Point of Confrontation. 2. Megalopolis: Is It Inevitable?" *Transactions of the Bartlett Society*, Vol. 3 (1965), pp. 9–22, 23–41; "Small Towns: A New Role for Old Communities?" *Redbook Magazine*, September 1965, pp. 20, 22; "Neighbourhoods and Human Needs," *Ekistics*, Vol. 21, No. 123 (February 1966), pp. 124–26; "A Cruise into the Past—and a Glimpse of the Future," *Redbook Magazine*, February 1966, pp. 30ff.; "What Kind of Fit?" *Ekistics*, Vol. 31, No. 186 (May 1971), pp. 329–30; "The Kind of City We Want," *Ekistics*, Vol. 34, No. 209 (April 1973), pp. 204–7; "Housing and the Community" (Sydney, New South Wales: Housing Commission of New South Wales, 1975); epilogue to Carlos C. Campbell, *New Towns: Another Way to Live* (Reston, Va.: Reston Publishing Co./Prentice-Hall, 1976), pp. 267–69; "At Home in the World—in New York," *New York*, December 20, 1976, pp. 8, 10; "Habitat," *Science*, Vol. 192, No. 4243 (June 4, 1976); and "Human Element in City Planning," *Ekistics*, Vol. 252 (November 1976), pp. 279–80.

9. Primary sources for Mead's views on race are *Blackberry Winter*, *A Rap on Race*, and *Science and the Concept of Race*. Additional sources include: "Race Majority—Race Minority," in Margaret Hughes (ed.), *The People in Your Life: Psychiatry and Personal Relations by Ten Leading Authorities* (New York: Knopf, 1951), pp. 120–57; "The Myth that Threatens America," in M. David Hoffman (ed.). *Readings in Democracy* (New York: Grove, 1952), pp. 101–5; "Breaking the Barriers of Prejudice," in *New Frontiers of Knowledge: A Symposium by Distinguished Writers, Notable Scholars and Public Figures* (Washington, D.C.: Public Affairs Press, 1957), pp. 30–32; "We've Got a Blending of Races Right Now," *U.S. News and World Report*, November 18, 1963, pp. 89–90; "Sense—and Nonsense—About Race," *Redbook Magazine*, September 1969, pp. 35ff.

The report "Equality Goals and Urban Progress" was prepared for the Goals for Metropolitan Areas Subcommittee (New York: June 2, 1966). For additional comments by Mead and her critics, see "Science and the Race Problem," *Science,* Vol. 142 (1963). pp. 558–61, with critiques of the AAAS Committee statement by Drs. Henry E. Garrett and Wesley C. George (pp. 913–15) and Carleton Putnam (pp. 1419–20).

The quotation about Ruth Benedict is from Mead's foreword to Benedict's *Race: Science and Politics* (New York: Compass Books/Viking, 1959), pp. vii–xi.

10. *Twentieth Century Faith* provides the fundamental statement of Mead's religious and ethical beliefs. Additional sources include: "The Liberal Church in an Urban Community," *Journal of the Liberal Ministry,* Vol. 4, No. 2 (Spring 1964), pp. 65–73; "Margaret Mead Answers . . . ," *Redbook Magazine,* September 1964, pp. 25–26ff.; "We Need a Religious System with Science at Its Very Core . . . ," *Look,* April 1, 1970, p. 37; "A Loyalty to the Whole World," *Yale Alumni Magazine,* Vol. 36, No. 2 (November 1972), pp. 16–17; "Dialogue on the Future" (with Roger Shinn), *Youth,* Vol. 23, No. 12 (December 1972), pp. 2–15; and "Summit V: One is the Human Spirit," in *One Woman's Voice* (New York: Anderson-Moberg Syndicates, October 1975).

For Mead's writings on birth control, see "Spiritual Issues in the Problem of Birth Control," *Pastoral Psychology,* Vol. 4, No. 34 (May 1953), pp. 39–44; and "Population Control: For and Against," in *Population Control: For and Against* (New York: Hart, 1973), pp. 52–68.

For readings on abortion, see "Margaret Mead Answers . . . ," *Redbook Magazine,* February 1963, pp. 21–22; "The Cultural Shaping of the Ethical Situation," in Kenneth Vaux (ed.), *Who Shall Live?* (Philadelphia: Fortress Press, 1970), pp. 4–23; and "Margaret Mead Answers . . . ," *Redbook Magazine,* July 1971, pp. 41, 44.

On sexual values, see "A Perfect Partnership," *Redbook Magazine,* February 1973, pp. 31ff.

On euthanasia, see "The Right to Die," *Nursing Outlook,* Vol. 16, No. 10 (October 1968), pp. 20–21; "Rights to Life," *Christianity and Crisis,* Vol. 32, No. 23 (January 1973), pp. 288–92; and "Margaret Mead Answers . . . ," *Redbook Magazine,* July 1973, pp. 33–34.

For her views on drug legalization, see "Margaret Mead Answers . . . ," *Redbook Magazine,* March 1963, pp. 28ff.; and "Drugs and Us," *Bazaar,* March 1971, pp. 130–31.

Civil disobedience is discussed in "Margaret Mead Answers . . . ," *Redbook Magazine,* January 1969, pp. 33, 35, and in Rabbi William Berkowitz (ed.), *Conversation with . . .* (New York: Bloch, 1976), pp. 163–89.

Mead wrote voluminously about the ethics of science, notably the following: "The Role of the Scientist in Society," in Lawson G. Lowrey and Victoria Sloane (eds.), *Orthopsychiatry 1923–1948: Retrospect and Prospect* (New York: American Orthopsychiatric Association, 1948), pp. 367–73; "Image of the Scientist among High-School Students: A Pilot Study" (with Rhoda Métraux), *Science,* Vol. 126, No. 3270 (August 30, 1957), pp. 384–90; "Closing the Gap Between the Scientists and the Others," *Daedalus,* Winter 1959, pp. 139–46; and "Man on the Moon," *Redbook Magazine,* July 1969, pp. 70ff.

11. Marvin Harris was quoted in *Time,* March 21, 1969, pp. 74–75. Wilton S. Dillon's paper is entitled "Shaping Structures for World Citizenship" (Boston: AAAS Annual Meeting, February 1976). Mead's comment about her optimism comes from "Margaret Mead Answers . . . ," *Redbook Magazine,* February 1972, pp. 45ff. Her statement about "just enough frost on the blackberries" is from an interview with Joan Wixen, "I've Always Been a Woman . . . I've Never Been an Imitation Man," *The Sunday News Magazine,* Detroit, June 22, 1975, pp. 12–13ff. The Jean Houston article in which Mead gave her epitaph is "The Mind of Margaret Mead," *Quest/77,* July/August, 1977, pp. 22–26ff.

Books by Margaret Mead

This bibliography of Mead's major works is arranged chronologically. Foreign editions or reprinted editions are not listed. The definitive bibliography, edited by Joan Gordan, is *Margaret Mead: The Complete Bibliography 1925–1975* (The Hague: Mouton & Co., 1976). A supplemental bibliography is available at the Library of Congress, where Mead's papers are stored.

Coming of Age in Samoa: A Psychological Study of Primitive Youth for Western Civilization. New York: Morrow, 1928.

An Inquiry into the Question of Cultural Stability in Polynesia. (Columbia University Contributions to Anthropology, Vol. 9.) New York: Columbia University Press, 1928.

Growing Up in New Guinea: A Comparative Study of Primitive Education. New York: Morrow, 1930.

"Social Organization of Manu'a," *Bernice P. Bishop Museum Bulletin,* 76. Honolulu, Hawaii, 1930.

The Changing Culture of an Indian Tribe. New York: Columbia University Press, 1932.

"Kinship in the Admiralty Islands," *Anthropological Papers of The American Museum of Natural History*, 34, No. 2 (New York, 1934), pp. 183–358.

Sex and Temperament in Three Primitive Societies. New York: Morrow, 1935.

Cooperation and Competition among Primitive Peoples. (Editor.) New York: McGraw-Hill, 1937.

From the South Seas: Studies of Adolescence and Sex in Primitive Societies. New York: Morrow, 1939.

Balinese Character: A Photographic Analysis. (With Gregory Bateson.) (Special Publications of The New York Academy of Sciences, 2.) New York: New York Academy of Sciences, 1942.

And Keep Your Powder Dry: An Anthropologist Looks at America. New York: Morrow, 1942.

Male and Female: A Study of the Sexes in a Changing World. New York: Morrow, 1949.

The School in American Culture. (The Inglis Lecture, 1950.) Cambridge, Mass.: Harvard University Press, 1951.

Soviet Attitudes Toward Authority. New York: McGraw-Hill, 1951.

Growth and Culture: A Photographic Study of Balinese Childhood. (With Frances Cooke Macgregor and photographs by Gregory Bateson.) New York: Putnam, 1951.

Cultural Patterns and Technical Change: A Manual Prepared by the World Federation for Mental Health. (Editor.) (Tensions and Technology Series.) Paris: UNESCO, 1953.

The Study of Culture at a Distance. (Editor, with Rhoda Métraux.) Chicago: University of Chicago Press, 1953.

Themes in French Culture: A Preface to a Study of French Community. (Editor, with Rhoda Métraux.) (Hoover Institution Studies, Ser. D, Communities No. 1.) Stanford, California: Stanford University Press, 1954.

Childhood in Contemporary Cultures. (Editor, with Martha Wolfenstein.) Chicago: University of Chicago Press, 1955.

New Lives for Old: Cultural Transformation—Manus, 1928–1953. New York: Morrow, 1956.

An Anthropologist at Work: Writings of Ruth Benedict. (Editor.) Boston: Houghton Mifflin, 1959.

People and Places. Cleveland and New York: World Publishing, 1959.

The Golden Age of American Anthropology. (Editor, with Ruth L. Bunzel.) New York: Braziller, 1960.

Continuities in Cultural Evolution. (The Dwight Harrington Terry Foundation Lectures on Religion in the Light of Science and Philosophy.) New Haven: Yale University Press, 1964.

Anthropology, A Human Science: Selected Papers, 1939–1960. (Preface.) (Insight Book, 22.) Princeton: Van Nostrand, 1964.

Anthropologists and What They Do. New York: Watts, 1965.

Family. (With Ken Heyman.) New York: Macmillan, 1965.

American Women: The Report of the President's Commission on the Status of Women and Other Publications of the Commission. (Editor, with Frances B. Kaplan.) New York: Scribner, 1965.

The Wagon and the Star: A Study of American Community Initiative. (With Muriel Brown.) St. Paul, Minn.: Curriculum Resources; Chicago: Rand McNally, 1966.

The Small Conference: An Innovation in Communication. (With Paul Byers.) (Publications of the International Social Science Council, 9.) Paris and The Hague: Mouton, 1968.

Science and the Concept of Race. (Editor, with Theodosius Dobzhansky, Ethel Tobach, and Robert E. Light.) New York and London: Columbia University Press, 1968.

Culture and Commitment: A Study of the Generation Gap. Garden City, N.Y.: Natural History Press/Doubleday, 1970.

A Rap on Race. (With James Baldwin.) Philadelphia and New York: Lippincott, 1971.

To Love or to Perish: The Technological Crisis and the Churches. (Editor, with J. Edward Carothers, Daniel D. MacCracken, and Roger L. Shinn.) New York: Friendship Press, 1972.

Blackberry Winter: My Earlier Years. New York: Morrow, 1972.

Twentieth Century Faith: Hope and Survival. New York: Harper & Row, 1973.

Ruth Benedict. New York and London: Columbia University Press, 1974.

A Way of Seeing. (With Rhoda Métraux.) New York: Morrow, 1974.

World Enough: Rethinking the Future. (With Ken Heyman.) Boston: Little, Brown, 1975.

Letters from the Field 1925–1975. New York: Harper & Row, 1978.

Aspects of the Present. (With Rhoda Métraux.) New York: Morrow, 1980.

Index

abortion, 145–46
Academy of Natural Sciences, 16
Academy of Religion and Mental Health, 12
Adams, Léonie, 16, 24
Addams, Jane, 73
adolescents, 62–63; generation gap, 63
American Academy of Arts and Letters, 11
American Anthropological Association, 11, 132
American Association for the Advancement of Science, 11–12, 132; Committee on Science in the Promotion of Human Welfare, 12, 132
American Association of School Administrators, American Education Award (1970), 16
American Association of University Women, 73
American family, the, 55–71; adolescents, 62–63; babysitters, 57; clusters, 71; communities, three-generation, need for, 70–71; divorce, problems of, 56–57, 65, 67; extended family, erosion of, 56; "The Family in the Future," 55–56; generation gap, 63–65; grandparents, bridge across the gap, 64–65,

67; marriage, 67–70; nuclear family, isolation of, 56, 58–60, 70–71; overpopulation and family size, 57–58; parents left to age alone, 66–67; prefigurative culture, 63–64; urbanization, 57
American Federation of Television and Radio Artists, 20
American Legion, 13
American Museum of Natural History, 12, 16, 63, 118; Studies in Soviet Culture, 45n
American national character, 48–53; aggression, 50–51; boastfulness, 51–52; competitiveness, 49–50; family, role of, 49; home town, fascination with, 49; pecking order rather than class structure, 50; Puritan ethic, belief in, 52–53; a "third-generation" society, 48–49
And Keep Your Powder Dry (Mead), 13, 48–53, 122
Anthropological Film Institute, 11
anthropology studies, new branches of: culture and personality, 44; culture at a distance, 45; national character, 43–44

169